ISLAND
CROSS-TALK

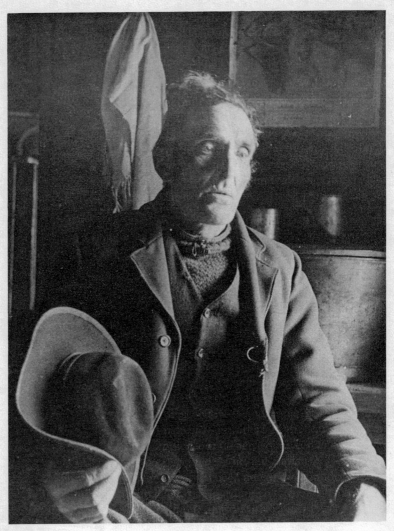

Tomás O'Crohan

TOMÁS O'CROHAN

ISLAND
CROSS-TALK

Pages from a Diary

TRANSLATED FROM THE IRISH
BY TIM ENRIGHT

Oxford   New York

OXFORD UNIVERSITY PRESS

Oxford University Press, Walton Street, Oxford OX2 6DP

Oxford New York Toronto
Delhi Bombay Calcutta Madras Karachi
Kuala Lumpur Singapore Hong Kong Tokyo
Nairobi Dar es Salaam Cape Town
Melbourne Auckland Madrid
and associated companies in
Berlin Ibadan

Oxford is a trade mark of Oxford University Press

Irish edition first published by
Government Publications, Dublin 1928
This edition first published 1986

English translation © Tim Enright 1986

British Library Cataloguing in Publication Data
Data available

Library of Congress Cataloging in Publication Data
Ó Crohan, Tomás, 1856–1937.
Island cross-talk.
Translations of: Allagar na hInise.
1. Blasket Islands (Ireland)—Social life and
customs. 2. Ó Crohan, Tomás, 1856–1937—Diaries.
I. Title.
DA990.B6502813   1986   941.9'6   85-15510
ISBN 0-19-281909-7

5 7 9 10 8 6 4

Printed in Great Britain by
Richard Clay Ltd.
Bungay, Suffolk

'Wouldn't it delight my heart to be able to read a book of my own before I died.'   Page 191

CONTENTS

Contents

LIST OF ILLUSTRATIONS

ACKNOWLEDGEMENTS

I HAVE to thank my wife Trudy for her help at every stage; Professor George Thomson, doyen of Blasket translators, for going through the manuscript and giving good advice; Revd Professor Pádraig Ó Fiannachta and Seán Ó Lúing from West Kerry, and Máire Guiheen from the Great Blasket for readily answering queries; and Nicola Bion of Oxford University Press for her patience and editorial care.

Photographs are by courtesy of Professors George Thomson and Tom Biuso; Walter McGrath and the 'Cork Examiner'; the Irish Folklore Department, University College, Dublin; Clódhanna Teoranta; and the Irish Tourist Board.

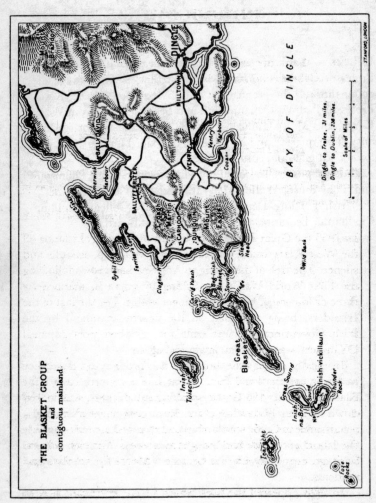

Map of the Blasket Islands

INTRODUCTION

Εσσεται ἦμαρ, ὅτ' ἄν ποτ' ὀλώλῃ Ἴλιος ἱρὴ
(The day will come when sacred Troy shall perish.)
Homer, *Iliad* vi. 448

Venit summa dies et ineluctabile tempus
Dardaniae. Fuimus Troes. Fuit Ilium et ingens
gloria Teucrorum.

(It has come, the final day, the hour which our Dardan land may not
evade. We Trojans are no more. Troy is no more and the great glory of
the Teucrians.)

Virgil, *Aeneid* ii. 324–6

In 1953 the Great Blasket, the largest of a group of islands off
the West Kerry coast, was abandoned to sheep, seagulls and
silence. The trek of the young to America had grown following
the First World War when fishing by currach, manned by
three or four men, became no longer viable. For the last of the
Islanders, being re-settled on the nearby mainland by the
Irish Government, it was exile too, as their poet Micheál
O'Guiheen was to lament again and again.

Ironically, by the time their story was brought to a close, they
had won international fame. Some half a century earlier the
Blasket, with its 150 Gaelic-speaking inhabitants, was looked
down on as an outlandish place. Resurgent nationalism and a
renaissance in Celtic scholarship had changed attitudes outside
the Island and inside had brought awareness of its rich cultural
heritage, especially when it became a Mecca for scholars and
students.

In 1928 appeared the book which I have attempted here to
render into English, *Allagar na hInise—Island Cross-Talk*, Pages
from a Diary—by a fisherman, Tomás O'Crohan. It was a
wonder to the Gaelic world for it had been written from within

the oral tradition, capturing the moment of transition from speech to writing. Living speech would be the hallmark of the series of books by Islanders which it was to inaugurate. Some, like the first, are classics which have been re-edited, and new editions of them are being prepared. The series has now grown into a small library, with translations into a number of languages, and books and articles about the Blaskets which continue to appear, alongside radio and television documentaries, seminars, lectures and talks.

Island Cross-Talk was a selection, approximately a third, from a diary Tomás O'Crohan wrote between 1918 and 1923. It was, with hesitation, undertaken at the suggestion of Brian O'Kelly from Killarney, a student of Gaelic, who had spent most of the year 1917 sitting at the feet of Tomás, titled 'the Master' by the other Islanders, themselves masters of their language and lore. Their culture was oral: story and song, poem, proverb, and prayer passed down by word of mouth from generation to generation. The poetry which they quoted at will helped to sharpen and refine their everyday speech.

Tomás, born as he tells us on St Thomas's day 1856, was taught English at the Island school but it was late in life that he learned how to read and write his own language. Now, out of fondness for his pupil who was leaving the Great Blasket and as a means of continuing their lessons together, he embarked upon the diary. Pens, ink, and paper were supplied by Brian O'Kelly to whom the manuscript was sent out in batches. When he understood the value of the material reaching him he suggested publication. As Tomás wrote:

I thought at first that it was because he wanted to be reading the language but he kept me at it for five years. He said it would be a great pity if I were idle, like the poet Seán O'Donlevy[1] long ago, and that I should write a couple of books while I had life in me, so as to live on after my death.

---

[1] A Blasket poet for whom Tomás had acted as scribe.

Tomás thought to amuse as well as instruct his pupil by recounting the cross-talk of Islanders whose quirks and oddities of behaviour and expression he had come to know during his stay. Comments on the weather, of daily concern on an island three miles out, often grew into lyrical descriptions of natural phenomena, penned simply and swiftly, his seabird's eye darting on the essential. Marcel Proust has written of *la tyrannie de la rime* which he says forces good poets into the discovery of their finest lines. With Tomás, unlettered in the accepted sense, it was the 'tyranny' of the pen. Said Brian O'Kelly:

Tomás is a writer, a fisherman, a farmer with one cow and a stonemason too. He handles words as he handles stones: he makes pictures with them. This book is a picture of the Western Island and a true picture. Therefore it is literature.

The talk he heard around him all day is refracted through the mind of the diarist, who is always humorously alert to the foibles of his fellows. The shafts fly at known targets and the retorts are expected. It is verbal fencing, in the cut and thrust of which the young join freely with the old. It is like, and often literally is, family banter, as between Séamas and his uncle Séamaisín. Séamas, with the words 'my dear—', 'sweet—', or 'darling man' for ever on his lips, is a cheerful man who always seems to be running out of the tobacco which he craves. This is a cause of irritation to Séamaisín, a choleric old man easily provoked to explosions of invective. Any seemingly chance remark might detonate these. Needless to say, they would be recounted and savoured by the Islanders.

And 'seemingly' is the word to keep in mind always when reading verbal exchanges within this close-knit community, homogeneous socially, culturally and economically. Humour is constantly bubbling on their lips. Along with their religion, it was one of the main buttresses against the storms of adversity which often battered their island home.

Humour too was a keynote of Tomás O'Crohan's second book, despite the sombre story he often had to tell. This was his autobiography *'An tOileánach'*—*The Islandman*[1]—the story of a community rather than biography in the traditional sense. It was Brian O'Kelly who urged him to undertake this, after he had served his apprenticeship on the diary. In a Foreword to *Island Cross-Talk* he explains:

> Before I went to the Blaskets Tomás used to write down old songs and folktales but he had no concern with what is normally termed literature. I urged him to write pieces about himself, the Islanders, or anything else he wished.
>
> 'Everyone knows what life is like here,' he rejoined.
>
> I asked him to write a story set in the Island but he demurred on the grounds that readers would believe it to be true. I got hold of, and read to him, 'Pêcheur d'Islande' *Iceland Fisherman* by Pierre Loti. However he preferred Maxim Gorky's stories which portrayed the harsh life of the people of Russia. Gorky showed Tomás that a fisherman could write a book as well as a learned man.

Once again Tomás O'Crohan astonished the Gaelic world, and *The Islandman* immediately established itself as a literary classic. Like the diary, it had been sent out in batches to Brian O'Kelly, who left Ireland for the Continent before it was completed. He placed both manuscripts in the hands of the West Kerry Gaelic writer and scholar Pádraig Sugrue, who had given him his first lessons in Gaelic before sending him on to continue his studies under 'the Master'. Sugrue persuaded Tomás to complete his story and he then edited both manuscripts for publication. Introducing *Island Cross-Talk*, he wrote of the diary:

> On reading it I soon discovered its uncommon character. It riveted my attention . . . here we have a peasant revealing his own mind and the traits of those about him according to his own background and experience. He has no knowledge of any other outlook or any other way of life, nor of any literary forms or rules for telling his story . . . In Tomás's writing there is truth, baldly expressed, an account without ornament and a completely accurate picture of a community

---

[1] Translated by Robin Flower, Oxford, 1951.

of people . . . which only a member of that community could fully understand.

This book is a voice from the Gaeltacht[1] itself . . . Tomás is of the Gaeltacht. He knows nothing else in the wide world. He never put a foot outside Corcaguiney, he never spoke anything but Irish, he never read anything of literature except a little recently in Gaelic. He has known nothing of a life of ease or of wealth from the day he was born, only of hard work and of few possessions. He understands the Gaeltacht, what is deep in its heart and the heart of its people. He is not conscious of this awareness, however, only as a bird is of its own song. It is displayed here in this book, in the way best known to a man not nurtured in learning and without literary training . . .

The reader must imagine that small, lonely island, the most western habitation in Europe, cut off from the life and knowledge of Europe . . . Of God's gifts what they have must be snatched through toil and constant peril from the mouth of sea and storm. He must imagine men and women reared in hardship and aware of the constant threat of poverty and hunger hanging over them. A little satisfies them and, when that little comes their way, they are the lively, cheerful, jesting people . . .

To them Ireland is a distant country. Springfield or Holyoke, Mass. is more of a capital city for them than any in the land of their birth. They have no newspapers, no library, no secondary school, only the learning that comes naturally to them, and which stamps their minds, from the constant intercourse with nature, with the pitiless beauty of the world, with the wildness and calm of wind and sea . . .

Tomás O'Crohan belongs to that community, at one with them in almost everything, except the uncommon gift he possesses of being able to commit his thoughts and reflections to the permanence of writing. He is an old man now, seventy-two years of age.

Tomás O'Crohan added two more volumes to the Blasket series: a topography of the Islands and a collection of lore. He also helped the Revd George Clune to compile his book of Blasket idiom:

Father Clune came and spent three weeks with me. He said Mass for us every day. He came back again, and I was a month in his company.

---

[1] Gaelic-speaking area, mainly along the western seaboard.

We helped one another, correcting all the words in 'Réilthíní Óir'. We used to be sitting at it eight hours a day in two sessions—four hours in the morning and four in the afternoon—for all that month. That's the most painful work I ever did, on land or sea.

Where Tomás pioneered others would follow. Maurice O'Sullivan wrote *Fiche Blian ag Fás—Twenty Years A-Growing*[1] —destined to be translated into English and other languages. The years a-growing were years a-glowing for youth on the Western Island but, at the end of the book brimming with *joie de vivre*, a shadow is cast. Maurice, instead of following other members of his family to America, had joined the Civic Guard, the new Irish police force. He returned on a visit to the Blasket:

There was a great change in two years—green grass growing on the paths for lack of walking; five or six houses shut up and the people gone out to the mainland; fields which had once had fine stone walls around them left to ruin; the big red patches on the Sandhills made by the feet of boys and girls dancing—there was not a trace of them now.

The same awareness that their world was passing away impelled Peig Sayers to tell her story in *Peig*[2] and in *Machtnamh Seana-mhná—An Old Woman's Reflections*.[3]

These authors were acutely aware of the values, above all cultural, of the old Gaelic world whose passing they mourned and which Greek scholars have compared to that of Homer. They were not aiming to preserve the memory of themselves or their fellow-Islanders as individuals but as representatives, pall-bearers rather, of that culture. At its heart lies the story-teller, but he needed an audience and that audience was being decanted to the next parish west—in Massachusetts.

As has been noted, the Islanders' awareness of their cultural heritage owed much to the scholars and students visiting them. Among these was Robin Flower, Assistant Keeper of Manu-scripts in the British Museum. He too had sat at the feet of 'the

[1] Translated by Moya Llewelyn Davies and George Thomson, Oxford, 1953.
[2] Translated by Bryan MacMahon, Dublin, 1974.
[3] Translated by Séamus Ennis, Oxford, 1962.

Master', whose translator he became. In his book *The Western Island*[1] he describes Tomás as

> a slight but confident figure. The face takes your attention at once and holds it. This face is dark and thin, and there look out of it two quick and living eyes, the vivid witnesses of a fine and self-sufficing intelligence. He comes towards you, and with a grave and courteous intonation, and a picked and running phrase, bids you welcome. You have indeed come home, for this is . . . the Island poet and story-teller.

Flower described Peig Sayers as 'a natural orator, with so keen a sense of the turn of phrase and the lifting rhythm appropriate to Irish that her words could be written down as they leave her lips, and they would have the effect of literature with no savour of the artificiality of composition'.

Peig's words were so written down by her son Micheál O'Guiheen, the last of the Blasket poets and storytellers, who acted as scribe for her books. He belonged to the next generation of Island authors, who also included Tomás O'Crohan's son Seán. They too would recount the customs and ways of the Island; they also told the story of its last days and how they resettled on the mainland from which their forebears had emigrated.

It was a remarkable harvest to spring from a book, the genesis of which had been a postal course in Gaelic: sixteen volumes by Islanders to which might be added a book of letters in English and an account, in Gaelic, by a teacher in the Island school, describing her days there. And it continues to give yield. A recent example is *The Blasket That Was* (An Sagart, Maynooth, 1982) by Professor George Thomson who had urged Maurice O'Sullivan to follow in the footsteps of 'the Master', and who had edited and helped to translate *Twenty Years A-Growing*. He writes of Pádraig Keane, 'the King', one of the characters in the diary:

> No special significance was attached to the title, which was regarded

[1] Oxford, 1944.

as a tribute to his fine physique and dignified bearing. Most of the old men had nicknames, and this was one of them. However, his position was an important one. He was the postman. Every Tuesday and Friday, weather permitting, he made the crossing to the mainland to despatch and collect the mail at the post-office in Dunquin. He had good English, and on his journeys to the mainland he represented the Islanders in any dealings they might have with the civic authorities.

The editor of the diary let the nicknames stand but, to avoid any possible offence, gave fictitious names for some of the characters. Such sensitivity hardly applies by this time. Séamas was Micheál O'Ġuiheen, brother-in-law of Peig Sayers, a bachelor who helped Peig to rear her family when her husband died at an early age. His uncle Séamaisín was Micheál O'Sullivan, brother of Maurice O'Sullivan's grandfather old Eoghan, who appears under his own name. So does Peig, who has been described as being 'like a woman from the Middle Ages'. Those who read her books will recognize how brilliantly Tomás captures the tone of her voice in the entry on page 44.

'Tadhg the Joker' was Seán O'Donlevy, described by Robin Flower as

a magnificent figure of an old man like one of the heroes of Irish story. He stands still, tall and vigorous, though he is an old age pensioner, and works all day long in the field with unremitting energy. A great nose juts like a rock out of his furrowed face, between one open and one drooping eye, above a big mouth out of which, when he speaks, there comes a tremendous roar of sound that almost deafens the hearer.

His wife Méiní—'Nell' in the book—was a celebrated story-teller, just as 'Séamaisín' was a celebrated singer.

It was the editor who supplied the apt title for the book and headings for the diary entries he chose. An examination of the much enlarged second edition, by Pádraig Malone in 1977, shows how representative his selection was.

Nine years after its publication the author of *Island Cross-Talk* died on 7 March 1937, aged eighty-one, on the Great Blasket Island where he had been born. He was aware by then of his stature as a Gaelic writer, and one of his books had been translated. In the diary he had expressed the wish: 'Wouldn't it delight my heart to be able to read a book of my own before I died.' This had been more than fulfilled, for he had placed his small island, three miles by one, on the literary map of the world. To commemorate the hundredth anniversary of his birth, a special stamp was issued. He was the first native-speaking Irish writer to be so honoured.

Tomás O'Crohan composed his own epitaph, and that of his community, when in *The Islandman* he wrote: 'the like of us will never be again'.

T. E.

Séamas and his Cravings

MEN working in the fields pause to take a break together. It is a lovely warm day. Some have sweat on them, some have a thirst and some have the cramp of laziness.

'Holy Mary, isn't it the parching day, men!' says Séamas.

'By my palms,' replies big Diarmaid O'Shea, 'if there's a dry taste in your mouth, boy, it is not for want of cured mackerel, and you to be so parched.'

'Upon my soul, my sweet man,' says Séamas, 'it is a long time since any change from salt fish went into my mouth, except the bitter pickle. No, 'tis the parching heat of the sun today and the little spell of work that are giving me this craving.'

'Isn't that the food you love best,' says Séamaisín, the argumentative man amongst them, 'for if you had been out fishing last night and had half a hundred of mackerel in the currach, you would rather take twopence for your share than put any in the pot for yourself.'

'Yerra, my hearty men,' says Séamas, 'it is seldom so many stop work but someone has his pipe reddened.'

'Let some decent man give the poor fellow a match,' Séamaisín says. 'Maybe he has a smoke in his pipe. "What is rare is wonderful".'

'My dear uncle, there's been no smoke in my own pipe for a week.'

'And may there not be another, for the length of your days!' says Séamaisín.

April 1919

The Call of the Cuckoo

'I HEARD the cuckoo today, upon my soul, whatever sign it is,' Tadhg the Joker says to his wife. 'I wonder, Nell, if anyone else heard it?'

'I know nothing whatever about that,' says she.

'You are not so blind about other matters that are no concern of yours at all,' says Tadhg.

'Aren't you in a great state over it. How well nothing crosses your path but it scalds you. You have to be different from everyone else in the village.'

'But, my dear woman, don't they say it's not a very good sign when anyone hears it at all; and I heard it clearly.'

'That depends on which direction it might be coming from. Was it from behind you heard the call? If so, that is no good sign.'

'Yerra, the devil, didn't I hear it in front and behind! And settle this question for me: it was calling in front when I faced uphill, but when I turned seawards, wasn't it calling behind me—so, my dear woman, 'tis hard for a man to be on his guard, if it means any harm.'

He set off westwards along the road and met a woman from the upper end of the village, drawing manure with an ass.

'Tadhg,' said she, 'the King heard the cuckoo today. I suppose nobody hears it except a King or a man of high rank like him.'

'God help us,' said Tadhg, 'you have relieved my mind of a great burden!'

End of April 1919

The Harsh Weather of Cuckoo Time

'THE harsh weather of Cuckoo Time is over, uncle,' said Séamas to Séamaisín.

'It is, wisha,' Séamaisín replied, 'and may it never return in full strength again. Many a man is sent to the Poorhouse by that selfsame month and, if I dare mention it, to the Madhouse too.'

'Holy Mary,' says Séamas, 'surely no one ever went to the Madhouse over it, whatever about the Poorhouse.'

'That is the notion of every simpleton like yourself that has not wit enough to read the signs of the world.'

'But I never heard yet that it sent anyone to the Madhouse.'

'You would have to be in the company of some man of sense for a while of the day to help you understand it,' says Séamaisín. 'Take the people who had the fruit of the year's work, all shades of green from every kind of seed showing above ground; after a day and a night of that harsh weather all they were left with in the morning was the bare earth. Some of those people ended up in the Madhouse rather than the Poorhouse itself.'

'By Our Lady, wisha, my darling man, today does not look too good either. Don't you see the fine blue-black ring round the sun since morning; and the day you see that, take to your heels from wherever you are,' says Séamas.

Séamaisín stares up.

'Bad luck to you up there for a ring!' says he. 'You are up to no good. 'Tis my opinion that the weather at hatching time for the hens will be as bad as it was at Cuckoo Time.'

Beginning of May 1919

The Pensioner's Sugar

'DID you hear what happened to the old age pensioner in the village here?' Tadhg of the Pranks asked.

'I did not, Tadhg.'

'Holy Mary, you are going to hear now! He is a man that always has the mad longing for sugar and he thought he could never get enough of it from Dunquin. When he had a sum of money saved he hoisted sail for Dingle to fetch a full sack of the sweetening that would last him a stretch of the year. The shopkeepers were gaping at him. He filled the sack with bags of sugar for himself, never mind the cost, though it is ninepence the pound.

'When he was satisfied he headed for home with his sack bulging. His wife emptied everything out onto the table. She removed the tea and suggested that the best thing would be to heap all the sugar together into the sack. That is what she did. She took a taste of it then and found it horrid. She had to spit it out.

'"There is an awful taste on this for sugar!" said she.

'"Oh, my heart to the devil! I had purgative for the cow in the sack and you have mixed it together!"

'"I have if it was there."

'"A shillings worth of salts," said he.

'"May the sweet devil sweep them between sack and cow!" said his wife.

'It had to be pitched out of the door,' said Tadhg.

May 1919

Manuring the Potatoes

'PEOPLE are earthing up the potatoes this year without any second manuring and that is something I never saw done before in this village, Séamas,' says Pádraig.

'You will see plenty that you never saw before if you live long enough,' says Séamas. 'Artificial manure from Dingle is what they are bringing back with them now, my sweet man, and great praise there is for it—that it yields better potatoes for eating than any other class of manure you can find.'

'Are ye going to bring any of it with ye?' asks Pádraig.

'Yerra, my darling man, all we can bring with us is misfortune—the full house of us there, God bless us! A pound a hundredweight that costs, my dear man, and then there is thirty shillings for a half sack of flour, ninepence for an ounce of tobacco, ninepence for a pound of sugar, a crown for a pound of tea—I leave clothes out of the count, for soon there won't be a stitch on any of us.'

'Ye'll be laid out from gathering mussels before ye'll have enough manure for all the potatoes ye have sown,' says Pádraig.

'Upon my soul, my sweet man, we have little heart or spirit for them.'

'What's holding ye back?' asks Pádraig.

'The hunger, wisha, seeing how I'm telling it to one of our own, and we for a month or more living on scraps since we gave up the sea, with only watery tea going into our bellies.'

While the pair were discussing these matters together, Séamaisín came along the path with a bag of mussels on an ass.

'You have been gathering mussels,' says Pádraig.

'I have. It was easy to gather them today with an ebb tide and calm there.'

'But here is a man who declares he could not gather any himself,' says Pádraig.

'Maybe he is not able to gather them,' says Séamaisín.

'Upon my soul, uncle, you have settled that question sharp enough. He declares he is short of enough to eat,' says Pádraig.

'Maybe that is no lie for him,' says Séamaisín, 'but seeing how he cannot find it in his heart to spend money for his needs in the shops, shouldn't he be content with a handful of mussels now and then as relish with the potatoes.'

'Séamaisín is the boy for you, Séamas,' says Pádraig.

'Wisha, seeing how no one got the better of him yet,' says Séamas, 'there is no use my making the attempt.'

Séamaisín left them there once he had that much off his chest.

May 1919

The Woman, the Seal and the Pensioner

A WOMAN drove her cow west in the early morning. When she had turned the cow into the field she thought it would not take her out of her way to pay a flying visit to the cliff above the strands. She was no feather-brain but a woman of sense who liked to lend a hand in her husband's work as well as her own. She looked down towards the shore and what was there but a big speckled seal below her on the high-water mark. A female it was, of huge girth.

She made her way down to see whether it was alive or dead. When she drew alongside she saw that it was sleeping. She flung a couple of stones at it. The seal lifted its head and let it droop again.

The woman scurried off to take the story home. When she came in sight of the fields she saw a man earthing up the potatoes with a spade. It struck her that this would make a good slaughtering weapon and she should get hold of it, so she chose to head straight for the workman. She explained how matters stood and what a useful weapon he had. She urged him to hurry and bring the spade. 'But, I dare say the seal will not be easy to kill in any case,' said the woman, who had never seen one like it on sea or land. 'There never was a greater hulk of a cow on this Island,' she declared.

He was a man who had been drawing the old age pension for four years and, although this author cannot title him warrior or hero, he saw himself in a different light. He shouldered his spade in high spirits that he would have a deed to boast about at the latter end of his days.

Off went the two of them instantly until they reached the cliff above the strand, but instead of the seal being on the high-water mark, as the woman had said, there was not its length between itself and the water now. The pair hurried on down.

An old seal would survive a blow from every man on this Island unless one of the blows struck his nose. When they drew alongside, said the woman:

'I had better grab it by the tail-end.'

'Yerra, the devil, that is what the woman did long ago, and the seal carried her off with no trace of her since,' said the man.

A single blow he dealt on the nose with the spade—that blow settled the seal.

'Wisha, "it is easy to know the blow of the veteran",' was the woman's comment.

Middle of May 1919

The Discontented Man

FEIDHLIM comes up to us. A miserable man this, covered in whiskers. He is frightened of the fairies and of people of flesh and blood too. Wind, sun or rain does not suit him. If someone came down from God's heaven looking for him to take him up there he would not go, for fear his own place might be better. He has the village plagued, and were it not for the way Tadhg the Joker puts him down, he would be a greater pest still. When he comes towards us he says:

'Well, 'tis here ye are.'

'We are.'

'Holy Mary, isn't it fine for ye. Ye're big and strong compared to the man collapsing to his knees trying to walk the pathway.'

'May you fall without rising,' says Tadhg, 'if it isn't feeble your croak is! How well 'tis always the same tale from you! A curse on Death seeing how he is leaving you in the throes for so long!'

'If he came, faith, and swept me off, wouldn't it be a blessing for me, rather than to be in this state with no life, or good, or use left in me,' says Feidhlim.

'May he grant you no further delay than tomorrow evening!' says Tadhg.

'Oh, Holy Mary, aren't you the wicked man to be railing at the likes of me. Isn't it small pity you have for me.'

'Yerra, you devil, haven't you the village plagued and every-one put off their work with all your moaning.'

May 1919

Girls Gathering Limpets

I WAS gathering mussels on a fine calm day. I had not been there long when I heard a voice behind me. I turned round to find a pair of young women nearby.

'Are there limpets here, Tomás?' one of them asked.

'There are, girl,' says I. 'Is it a fistful you want?'

'It is,' she said.

'What implement have ye for scraping them off?'

'I have the broken half of a pair of shears. The other girl has an iron bolt, but the limpets aren't too plentiful here.'

'Why didn't ye send yeer mothers to gather them? Wouldn't they have more skill and craft for the work?'

'But how would we ever learn if they always came to gather them?' said she. 'Holy Mary! Isn't it grand to be here by the sea's edge at low tide! The lovely smell that's there when everything that was under the sea before is under the sun now and its mouth gaping. I dare say the people of Dublin would love to be here at this time.'

May 1919

Otters and Seals

AT this time I was taking my ease out of the heat beside a field wall. I gazed round at sea and land and my eye fell on black shapes floating in the water. They were no great wonder to me as they might be to another man, for I often saw them before. They were otters, six altogether—the full-grown pair and four pups. It was not the habit of the Islanders here in the old days to call any woman a 'lady' unless she had an otter's skin round her neck or arm. An otter's skin fetched a good price at that time. The skins of those six were worth thirty pounds—five pounds apiece.

When they had moved off past me, a pair of huge speckled seals came behind them along the same path through the low water and a baby seal with them. The seal always had but the one offspring at a time. The otter, like the dog on land, has from three to six.

Many a man came visiting this Island and no matter if he had gold chains dangling from him, he was no proper gentleman, my friend, unless he wore a seal-skin waistcoat. This was a great resource for the Islanders in the old times. Neither otter nor seal is brought home now, nor for many a day. More of life's changes.

May 1919

Building Bell's House

MYSELF and another mason whose name is Dónall Kennedy were building Bell's house. Some men came up to us.

'Isn't it a great disgrace for ye to be working when there has been a death in the village,' they said.

They are forever taking a rise out of people with that sort of comment, so we paid as little attention to their flim-flam this day as any other. Asses were drawing turf at the time and a man here and there was working in the fields. It was not long before others came up to us. Séamas was with them.

'What great changes for the worse there are on this Island, Kennedy!' he said.

'What makes you say so?' the other man asked.

'Oh, a death in the village and there never was a day for work like it, my dear man,' said Séamas.

He was referring to the death of a year-old girl. Some people had stopped work, while others continued through the day. Since we were engrossed in the work on the house and there was a hurry with it, we stayed on. After dinner men went up past us with spades on their shoulders.

'Where are they going?' Kennedy asked.

'Cutting turf,' someone answered.

'And why are they idle since morning and going to work now?'

'The funeral is over now,' Séamas said, 'and she is buried.'

June 1919

Shearing the Sheep

SHEEP were being sheared on the strand, where they were packed tight after being brought down from the hill. Séamas paid a visit to view the spectacle and, since he had none of his own, he was highly critical of sheep and owners alike.

'Holy Mary, my sweet man, no wonder those fellows are so prosperous,' said he. 'They have the wool and the mutton and the lamb. The rest of us have no business to be in the world at all while their share of grass is being cropped by other people's sheep year in and year out.'

Séamaisín arrived on the scene, holding bags for wool and shears for cropping.

'Ye have sheep in plenty today, God bless ye, uncle,' said Séamas.

Now Séamaisín is a prey to superstition, and in dread of the evil eye and of boasting, so he blazed up in anger at Séamas because his words did not suit.

'Is it how ye haven't any share of them?'

'We have not, wisha, my sweet man. And it is a long time since we did,' Séamas answered.

'May ye be always in the same state!' said Séamaisín. 'It beats me how you could ever own anything, when you have nothing better to do than run from one man to the next, seeing who will spend the most time blathering with you.'

He hurried on his way down.

'Bad luck go with you!' said Séamas.

June 1919

Tomás O'Crohan and his son Seán

The Blaskets from Sliabh an Iolair

Hustle and Bustle

MEN have set out east and west; one currach is at Tiaracht fishing for lobsters and two are in Dingle, one with lobsters, the other with mackerel. The latter sell for four shillings the hundred and lobsters for a shilling apiece. A currach from Dunquin has gone west to Inishvickillaun with a gentleman on board—a man who is learning Gaelic in Comineol, like Brian[1] long ago. There are some people gathering turf, others are at school and others again are by the hearth, cooking for themselves—they have the best of it, I believe. They will have the tasting of everything.

When the men meet together around midday they ask each other the news.

'Were you out fishing last night, Séamas?'

'I was, my sweet man.'

'Did you have a good catch?'

'Two boats caught more than we did and two caught less. Six hundred we had.'

'Well, if you were short of relish with the potatoes for part of the year,' says Tadhg, 'maybe you haven't that to say today. It will be a long time now before you are so short of something tasty.'

'Upon my soul, my darling man, ten of them was all I brought home because we had no salt to preserve them,' says Séamas, 'and I let the two hundred of my share go to Dingle to pay for the salt. It is not the end of the world yet, with God's help.'

June 1919

---

[1] Brian O'Kelly. See Introduction.

Tadhg, Nell and the Ass

TADHG stuck his head out.

'The day is grand and dry, Nell,' said he, 'and I had better go in search of the ass and stack the handful of turf that is on top of the hill.'

'If you like.'

'Bad luck to him, looking for him and finding him are not the same thing at all!' he said.

'Head westwards along the north coast, that's where you'll most likely find him.'

At that he picked up his stick and strode off out of the house. He was gone for most of the day, and no sign of him or the ass returning.

'Mary, Holy Mother,' says Nell, 'isn't himself a long while coming, whatever about the ass.'

Her thoughts were soon interrupted when someone brought the news that the ass was below to the south, out on a ledge in the cliff. 'The hunter was west and the hound east.' Tadhg was north and the ass south.

There was nothing for it then but to head south herself, and when she reached the spot where the ass was, she saw that he was as far down the cliff as he could go. She set about scrambling down towards him, and that she was able to do, but what she could not do was come back up.

Tadhg arrived home and he was barely inside the door when a youngster rushed in to tell him that Nell and the ass were on the ledge.

'May the pair of them never come up!' he said.

Off he went, all the same, taking a rope to rescue them —which he did with help from the neighbours.

July 1919

A Circus Day with the Ass

ON Sunday currach races, and many other sports, were held in Paróiste Múrach. No one from this Island crossed over for them, but on Monday we had our own race here with Tadhg's half-blind, black ass, an occasion as full of fun and merriment as there has been in Ireland for a good while, I believe. Instead of this ass being broken in, they have no control over him at all by now, because his master is like an army major or an admiral on the high seas, his bark is so harsh. The result is that the ass, even if Tadhg is saying his prayers, senses some threat to himself and stands shivering in his skin in dread of him.

This Monday past, Tadhg drove him down from the hill around breakfast time, but when the ass found himself among the houses no one could catch up with him.

Tadhg roared and bawled for someone to stop the ass at every corner and crossing. The entire village heard him and out they ran.

His own family was everywhere trying to head off the ass. Nell was standing in his path with her two arms outstretched. The ass gave one bound, clearing both arms and body. He started off up the hill once more despite the efforts of everyone there.

If there was ever a circus day to beat it on this Island, I don't remember it.

July 1919

Gaelic Enthusiasts in Dingle

'HAVE you any news from Dingle, Pádraig?' asks Séamaisín.

'Nothing much, except that it is full of people mad for Gaelic—the streets are thronged. There would be as many more again except that no room could be found for them.'

'By Our Lady,' says Séamaisín, 'I dare say 'tis more harm they are doing than good. The town is eaten out by them and goods are dear as a result.'

'There are some who are thankful to them and others who are not,' says Pádraig. 'They are paying the lodging-house keepers well and bringing profit to the shopkeepers.'

'Never mind that,' Séamaisín says, 'but aren't goods dear for the country people on account of them. People thronging to shop in the town send the prices soaring everywhere.'

'That may well be,' says Pádraig, 'but no matter who came, some people would resent them. They say that soldiers will soon be stationed there as an expense on the place.'

'The devil take them too! What do they want there?' says Séamaisín. 'If they come here there won't be a soul left alive in the barony.'

July 1919

The Lobster Boat

'THE lobster boat is making from the south through Dingle Bay, sure as I'm alive,' says Tadhg. 'I was drawing a load of turf and 'tis she that's coming for a certainty and she'll be here soon.'

Before long she nosed past the Point and dropped anchor. Off they all went at a rush with their own catch, but it was crayfish that were wanted and lobsters were refused.

'Is the boat buying well, Séamas?' asked old Eoghan.

'Bad cess to it, my dear man,' says Séamas, 'it is not, nor anything like it. We have put the lobsters back into the pots again. The captain would make no offer at all for them, high or low.'

'Isn't that fellow a Corkman?' says Tadhg. 'And haven't you heard for long enough that they are the worst crowd in Ireland.'

'But he was given his notice never to come to this coast again,' says Séamas.

'May Satan sweep that fellow from you!' says Tadhg. 'He is the bad buyer.'

'Life was good up to now, if beggary isn't to be the end of ye,' says Séamaisín.

'Upon my soul, uncle, my sweet man,' says Séamas, 'it is beggary we'll come to before long. We have not been far off it ever since the day the lobster company failed us.'

August 1919

'*Off with Us to the Races!*'

IT is the day of the races in Ballyferriter parish. There isn't a soul in this village but has crossed over for them. However, we have no currach racing for us.

'Mary, Holy Mother,' says Séamas, 'isn't it the great wonder that we cannot muster four good men on this Island that would challenge them up north, though the Islanders can't be short of experience and they don't look like weaklings either.'

'They are weakhearted,' says Tadhg. 'If they didn't win the race up there they would die of the disgrace.'

'They would be taking a risk in any race for they are too fond of the race for drink,' says Séamaisín, 'and the day you fill your belly with that, stay out of it unless it was a race for old women and, by Our Lady, even they would beat you.'

'Off with us to have a look at them so,' says Séamas, 'if we can't have a race we'll have a drink.'

'Bad scran to you,' says Séamaisín, 'if you had any respect for yourself you wouldn't go spending your money there when nobody from your own place is entered to win the race. If there wasn't somebody from my own village in one of the races, I'd sooner take my money and pitch it over a cliff.'

'By Our Lady, wisha, uncle,' says Séamas, 'we'll have our pint, the day being what it is, if it's the last thing we do.'

'May that be the pint that chokes you!' says Séamaisín.

August 1919

The Day after the Races

THE currachs are coming back after the races. The news they brought was that no currach had raced. There had been rain all day, so the event would take place the following Sunday.

'There will be porter there, whatever about any race,' says old Eoghan.

'Oh, I dare say no one from this village will be there next week,' says Tadhg, 'they will be satisfied with what they drank the first day.'

'Wait a while,' says Eoghan. 'The day hasn't come yet.'

'Any news from Ballyferriter above, Séamas?' Tadhg asks.

'There is, wisha, my sweet man,' says Séamas, 'and it is not good news. They have neither potatoes nor oats. The drought left them all parched through and through.'

'Were there many people there?'

'I never saw such crowds,' says he. 'The pint of porter cost a shilling and everything else just as dear.'

'All those fat pigs they used to have—they'll not have so many now,' says Eoghan.

'They will not, my sweet man, nor cows nor horses either.'

'Ye took yeer time about coming back,' says Tadhg.

'Yerra, the weather was bad that night, so we took our ease above and stayed there until today,' says Séamas.

August 1919

Fishermen Eating Lobsters

'LOBSTERS are being brought home by the Islanders for their own table. These are some of life's changes, uncle, my sweet man,' says Séamas. 'What used to be caught for the bigwigs of England, and they gave a good price for them—to think we are eating them ourselves today.'

'But haven't ye been seeking Home Rule for a long while,' says Séamaisín, 'and isn't this one result of it. And soon it will be the same with the cattle as with the fish and that will be another result of it. All the tasty morsels the English used to be eating out of yeer mouths and yeerselves left without any decent bite at all—wasn't that yeer complaint always? But it was easy to see that some change was coming and ye would be eating well. It is a while since ye ate fine food; ye let that go to make the penny.'

'Upon my soul, my darling man,' says Séamas, 'whether we ate well or badly, we were never brought to this pass—the day the fisherman won't have a penny for his catch he will have neither bit nor bite and he'll be facing beggary.'

'Faith, a good lobster is no bad diet for you; and if you have a good sheep, kill that too. If you have a good heap of potatoes to go with them, to my way of thinking you have never known what it is to eat well until then,' says Séamaisín.

'By Our Lady,' says Tadhg, 'however much they deserve to be praised, his supply would soon run out and that would be the case with everyone. And if that is to be the result of the laws of Home Rule, may the devil sweep them out of the laws of the world!'

'Upon my soul, my dear boy,' says Séamaisín, 'there may be another small shift for the worse to come. "Every start is weak". I'm afraid the rule of the Englishman will be mourned yet.'

'Bad cess to you for a little ruffian,' says old Eoghan. 'If having good food instead of the bad the English allowed would make you shed tears over them, may it not be long before tears are shed over you at your wake!'

'The truth is,' says Séamaisín, 'if the laws came down from heaven, some of us would find fault.'

September 1919

Carters on Strike

THE currachs bring in the news that the Dunquin carters were on strike, because the buyers have cut the rate for carting the hundred fish to Dingle to half what it was last year.

'By Our Lady,' says Tadhg, 'we haven't known what misfortune was until this, or what are poor men to do now? However high or low the price for fish, it is worse still for it to be left behind on the cliff top.'

'Since they have the law laid down, it is very difficult to break,' declared old Eoghan. 'And the packers are charging a shilling a hundred for loading it to the cliff top; three shillings a hundred for carting it to Dingle—that is four shillings a hundred. There is nothing for it but to stay at home and not go out fishing at all.'

'Let poor men pick up the bag so, my darling man,' says Séamas, 'and be ready to go begging for charity and, by Our Lady, there will be none of that for them to get, I dare say.'

'By Our Lady,' says Tadhg, ''twas said there was many a reason for starting the Great War, but the only reason there ever was for starting it was to kill off this Island.'

'Ireland was never in such a state until this strike, my sweet man,' says Séamas. 'With the Dunquin drivers on strike, you could cart no fish to Dingle today, even if you had it.'

'My curse on them!' says Tadhg, 'they are the very worst who ever loaded the fish up.'

'If ye would only salt the first of the fish, it would be a great help in bringing them back to their senses,' says Eoghan.

'Yerra, my sweet man,' says Séamas, 'that is something you could never do in this village. Ten shillings for a hundredweight of salt, more trouble curing the fish, and another thing to be taken into account, my sweet man, no horse and cart to be had to fetch the hundredweight of salt for you, since the devil got into the carters, and they being paid handsomely already. But 'tis how if they keep this up, there soon won't be a soul left alive in Ireland.'

'It is hard for the poor people to bear,' says Tadhg. 'Four pounds for a net and thirty pounds for a currach. Twelve shillings for a pound of tea and four pounds of sugar. Close on a shilling for an ounce of tobacco!'

September 1919

Food Ships Idle

'This is the worst year for potatoes in a long time—with us at any rate,' says Eoghan.

'The blight is on them in many places,' says Tadhg, 'but whatever about anywhere else, the ones here taste of seaweed.'

'Even the oats are rotten,' says Séamas, 'and that's no wonder, my darling man, never-ending rain day after day with no sign of the sun from Monday to Saturday. The world is in bad shape ever since the Great War and I'm afraid it won't improve.'

'By my baptism,' says Tadhg, 'it was the grand life until it came to an end—'tis now it has gone to the devil. But my own belief is that all the misfortune in the place is the fault of those strikers.'

'Isn't it a great wonder that the Government isn't reining them in,' says Séamaisín.

'Yerra, man,' says Tadhg, 'isn't that what these fellows want? The more trouble they cause, the more they'll bring the country down.'

''Tis no good news that came in today, uncle,' says Séamas.

'What's troubling you now?' asks the uncle.

'It is this, my sweet man: the big ships that were piled high with goods of all kinds have left the harbours of Ireland again, as laden as they were when they sailed in.'

'But why ever so?' asks the uncle. 'It seems to me that what they brought is badly needed.

'Something wicked got into them,' says he.

'The devil got into them, God save us,' says Séamas, 'to say that people didn't pull together to store away the food for themselves, at least. If there was any sensible way of doing things today, they would put a stop to it tomorrow.'

'I suppose another strike is on,' says Tadhg, 'that caused

them to go away again but, by Our Lady, it is likely the strike would have petered out by the time they were sent for to unload the next ship.'

'I suppose seven full years of your life will have gone past before you see any other full ship in any harbour in Ireland after this work,' says old Eoghan, 'and if John Bull's men were the cause of all this, you'd never hear the end of it in Ireland.'

September 1919

Seal Meat or Pig Meat

'Wasn't the spring tide fine and calm for killing seals, no stir on any rock and a grand ebb there,' says Tadhg.

'They're gone from the world, my sweet man,' says Séamas, 'like much else besides, though someone yesterday was paid the fine sum of a pound for the skin of one.'

'Who got the money and who paid it?' asks Eoghan. 'I think you often tell a tall story.'

'Seán Mhichíl got it and the gentleman staying up at Donncha's house paid it, but he was given a seal pup into the bargain.'

'Upon my soul, but 'twas the great life of it when we were eating them,' says Eoghan, 'for they were as good to eat as the pig costing two shillings a pound today.'

'You're without pig and without meat since you gave up hunting them,' says Tadhg, 'for you can't afford the pig and that's why God put the seals there in place of pigs for the poor, to help them eke out a living.'

'I'm afraid they'll be hunted again yet,' says Séamaisín, 'if life gets any harder.'

September 1919

Blasket Village

The Island and corn stooks

Yanks from the Island in Dingle

''Tis said that Yanks from the Island have arrived in Dingle,' says Séamaisín.

'Who said so?' asks Tadhg.

'The Dunquin people. The currach that went there with fish today brought the news.'

'Yerra, curse that crowd! Aren't they the greatest liars on God's earth,' says Tadhg. 'The last currach that put out from the Island is gone to Dingle. They'll have the full story when they come back and I will bet there is no truth in the rumour.'

'There's a curse on America if this place is any better,' says Séamas, 'but, my sweet man, you're better off working anywhere but where you'd be under somebody's eye day in and day out.'

'Don't you know that wherever that is going on, it is a corner of hell,' says Séamaisín, 'and that is what the place yonder is too, judging by the way people who come back from there go without sleep or rest in their struggle to make a living.'

'But they have good pay in Ireland now,' says Séamas.

'The good pay in Ireland won't last because they can't keep on paying it,' says Séamaisín.

September 1919

Hunting Wild Geese

PÁIDÍN O'SHEA went to Inishvickillaun with a few sheep. As he drew near the island what did he see in the water but a flock of geese in front of him—a great number of them. He set off in pursuit, rowing flat out. He picked up a good many—nearly a currach full—but he had to leave many more behind, for he couldn't catch up with them. The goose is a powerful swimmer while he has the strength.

Early next morning six currachs took up the search but failed to find them. They had lobster pots too which they wanted to bring home. It must have been after midday that some people herding cows saw the geese from the hill—a whole flock of them. The currachs set off to give chase—four of them, rowing furiously, but they had to call it off and return home without a single goose.

'You brought no goose back after the chase, Tadhg,' said Séamas.

'The sweet devil sweep them from me! I did not, my dear man,' said Tadhg.

September 1919

Currachs Caught in a Storm

THE currachs were out fishing. The night was very blustery. Some of them reached the Island early in the night, but others took refuge from the storm in the shelter of Beiginis. They had some fish already and they were counting on the storm abating so that they could add to their catch. Instead it blew harder than ever. They had to stem the current beside Beiginis until day brightened—three currachs from the Island and five from the mainland. At daybreak they were unable to land on the Island or over on the Dunquin side either. They had to run before the weather and head for Ram's Creek. At the landing place there it was calm. They hauled up the Dunquin boats. The three Island currachs headed for home through the squall. Everyone in the village was gazing out at them and the swell towering above them. The tide was in their favour. Only for that they would not have won the day.

'Holy Mary,' said Séamas, who was down at the slip when they landed, 'they are the best boats in the world! A ship would have had a struggle to do the work they did.'

'Mind you, it is not a choppy sea they are facing and the tide is with them,' said Séamaisín.

September 1919

The Herb Séamaisín would Sell his Shirt for

'WHAT price did the fish make today, Séamas?' asks Séamaisín.

'Twelve shillings, my sweet man.'

'It was not worth more—fish not even the size of my little finger for the most part.'

'That may be so, uncle,' says Séamas, 'but there were some that were the length of my arm.'

'Upon my soul, they would have to be, for if they were all as small they wouldn't be worth half a crown,' says Séamaisín.

'Isn't it a great market, my sweet man,' says Séamas, 'compared to the pound of tea costing the same.'

'Bad scran to you, if you compare your pound of tea with your lump of a mackerel! when there isn't a herb growing anywhere I would sell the shirt off my back for, only that one,' says Séamaisín. 'You would be a long while eating mackerel before you would start dancing for me. The tea is a different matter —after you've swallowed that you would be skipping about like a goat.'

'By Our Lady, uncle, in that much at least I would agree with you. I would have gone to eternity long ago, my darling man, only for all of it I have swallowed, that's my belief.'

'It would be little harm if no one died for want of it only yourself! But I dare say there would be many more with the same disease', says Séamaisín.

October 1919

The Fine Potatoes Last Year

'WHAT are yeer potatoes like, Máire?' asks Peig. 'I wonder if they are as bad as my own?'

'Whatever yeers are like,' says Máire, 'they're small, black and sparse with us, my dear, and on top of that there is no taste of food or fare on them.'

'Holy Mary! wasn't it the grand crop last year?' says Peig. 'So full of white flour that you wouldn't want any bread, just them on their own and swallow your mug of tea down afterwards.'

'If they were like white flour for the past four years,' says Máire, 'we had plenty of the black flour too.[1] How in the world did anyone live on it?'

'It wasn't the black flour they depended on, my darling,' says Peig, 'but on those fine potatoes, and there's grand flour this year, now that the potatoes are poor. We should be thankful to God who orders everything the right way.'

'I wonder, Peig, was it He that caused the Great War to be fought?'

'Yerra, bless you, I dare say He is the cause of everything. Isn't He the Master? And much will have to happen to thin out the human race to make room for those to come,' is Peig's reply.

October 1919

---

[1] A reference to war-time flour.

The Price of Fish

'Isn't this the cold and wet weather we have, Tadhg,' says Eoghan. 'It has a curse down on top of it entirely but, as the old saying goes, Michaelmas is the time the weather breaks for good and there never was a truer word. The weather turns threatening from then on.'

'It is no very good weather for fishing, though their catches have been fair,' says Tadhg. 'They would not have caught as many maybe if the weather had been calm.'

'Maybe they would not, and maybe they would have caught nothing whatever,' says Eoghan. 'Calm doesn't suit the fish that's there now at all. It is better in unsettled weather, that's when it surfaces.'

'What price did it fetch yesterday?' asks Tadhg.

'Sixteen shillings, and it will soon reach the pound, I suppose,' says Eoghan, 'and you would think during the year that there was no profit in it. Is fair day long from us?'

'Saturday coming. That is the Michaelmas fair, I suppose,' says Tadhg.

'It is to be sure,' says Eoghan. 'There was never fine weather around that time.'

October 1919

Tadhg's Ass Again

'TADHG,' says Nell, 'there isn't a single turnip left in the field by the crowd looking out for the currachs by night.'

'It's a wonder the devils aren't afraid,' says Tadhg, 'when there's a steep drop on every side of them, that someone might come and pitch them over. Is that old stump of an ass around so that I can go and draw a load of turf with him?'

'I never laid an eye on him this day.'

'Yerra, isn't it only now I sent him down the road myself.'

'But if you did, he never came as far as the house,' says Nell.

Tadhg dashed off after him again and he soon found him in the fields. He and the ass turned for the house once more. A man met him on the path and the pair of them swopped talk for a while, but when Tadhg reached the house a second time there was no ass ahead of him.

'Where's the ass now, Nell,' said he, 'till I put the straddle on him? The day is well melted on me.'

'The ass never set foot here today, man.'

'If he didn't, may he never come again!' said Tadhg. 'Let the house go without food and fire so!'

October 1919

Dogfish in the Sea

'HASN'T the snow come early this year,' says Eoghan, 'and the potatoes that have been lifted will go bad under it I suppose.'

'They say it does harm to them,' says Tadhg, 'and it is not a good sign for it to be coming so soon.'

'Oyeh, it is a year of foul, unsettled weather altogether, man, with no fine spell in it, only constant rain and wind,' says Séamaisín. 'Signs on it, the land has given little yield.'

'Wasn't it a poor catch they had last night,' says Eoghan. 'I believe they had to run home on account of the dogfish.'

'That's what they'll face from now on unless they are very lucky,' says Séamaisín. 'There's no net made, sure, that wouldn't be bitten through by them in a single hour.'

'Isn't it a great wonder that such evil creatures were created in the sea to do people harm,' says Eoghan.

'But is it how there are no creatures just as evil on land?' asks Séamaisín.

'There are, my dear man, if it's people you mean—they're not too good, some of them. But I suppose that is the way the world was created,' says Eoghan.

October 1919

How was the Fair?

'How was the fair, Yank?' Eoghan asks the Yank when he returns from Dingle fair. 'Are the market prices still as high as they were during the war?'

'No, nor half that! Cattle were well down in price, boy, and sheep and piglets. There's talk about nothing but fish. The bellman was out during the day in Dingle, announcing that buyers from America would be here soon, able to give a shilling a pound for mackerel.'

'It is good news that the Dingle people are thwarted, they never were the best buyers. Now maybe they will get their fingers burnt over their own share of it.'

'There never was a year for fish like it, they say,' answers the Yank. 'The barrel is being bought up as soon as it is full, to be sent overseas.'

'That looks promising,' says Eoghan. 'I suppose they had a poor catch in America this year, to say they're paying so much for it. What are the prices like in the shops?'

'As dear as they have ever been,' says the Yank.

October 1919

Fleeing from Seals

YOUNG O'Shea and two others went west to Inishvickillaun in
search of pollock. It was the ebb of a spring tide. They went in
towards a seal-cave where seals were to be found in large
numbers. The men had no stick or rod, for they only went to
have a look at them. There were sixteen full-grown seals there
and the same number of young ones. The bold Páidín
approached them and, as they have their own sense and are
always pitting their wits against man in various ways, what do
you think they did? Perceiving that Páidín had no weapon for
killing or for defending himself, they chased after him all over
the shore. The other two had hauled up the currach to dry land
by this time and they had to run to Páidín's aid—one with the
currach's mast and the other with an oar. The old seals took
flight then to the end of the cave, while others were escaping to
the sea. They took away the three best of the young seals in the
cave, not for their own use, but to barter for potatoes or oats with
the mainland people.

October 1919

Fish Shoaling

'WHAT a sight of fish there are shoaling today,' says old Eoghan.

'Yes, wisha, my darling man,' says Séamas, 'as many as ever I laid eyes on and they say it is a sign of a change in the weather when they are taking leave of their senses like that.'

'May the Saints take leave of you, you fool!' says Séamaisín. 'Don't you know that the fish shoal according to their own instincts, whatever the weather.'

'There'll be no one catching any fish tonight,' says Séamas.

'Sorrow to your heart!' says Séamaisín, 'you know everything! Surely they have a better chance of a catch than when there isn't any to be seen at all.'

'There is a glut of it. It only fetched ten shillings today,' says Séamas. 'That's a big drop from thirty, uncle.'

'Ye are used to getting top prices,' says Eoghan. 'I sold a deal of it in my time for half a crown and three shillings.'

'Peig, bring me out a mug of your water. I'm dying with the thirst since morning,' says Séamas.

'What's the cause of that?' asks Eoghan.

'I ate a small scad, well-pickled, this morning.'

'Couldn't you have treated yourself to a bit of meat after selling all the mackerel you caught,' says Eoghan.

November 1919

Ireland's Freedom

'WHAT brings that currach out?' asks Séamaisín.

'It is Seán Eoghain taking a bullock across. There's another man with him going out for flour,' answers Séamas. 'The currachs had no fish today and I suppose the fish will be asleep for a while now. It was never caught so late in the year, night after night, to my knowledge.'

'Is there any talk about the freedom of Ireland, Diarmaid,' asks Séamas, 'or where is Ireland's envoy[1] these days? Is he still in America?'

'The schoolmaster says he is, travelling from place to place. He is in California now,' Diarmaid Bán answers. 'The biggest wonder is the amount of money collected for him.'

'The money is a great boon,' declares Séamaisín. 'It will be a help for somebody.'

'It is for the freedom of Ireland,' says Diarmaid.

'That same freedom has me deafened and I don't know what it means,' says Séamaisín.

'We to have our own King here and the connection with England to be broken,' Diarmaid answers.

'I understand now,' says Séamaisín. 'One crowned King of England and another crowned King of Ireland—that's something you'll never see, Diarmaid, so long as the sun is in the sky. If there is a crown on a King in Ireland it will be England's crown he will have to wear.'

'I hope you're proved wrong!' says Diarmaid Bán.

November 1919

---

[1] Éamonn de Valera.

'When they have no Fish they will still have Sheep'

'Isn't it powerful money sheep are fetching now,' says Séamaisín. 'Six pounds a pair—five for a pair of poor quality. A great number of them have been shipped out from the Island these days.'

'They have grand weather for it,' says Eoghan.

'They are prospering—when they have no fish they will still have sheep,' says Séamaisín, 'but a man without sheep is without the means one way or another of making money out of them. Any man without a stock of sheep is not worth talking about—one to shear, one to sell and one to eat.'

'Nobody worth a light is without sheep either,' declares Eoghan. 'They cost nothing to keep and they will always bring in the penny.'

'Weren't they the early boats from Dunquin at the harbour this morning,' says Tadhg.

'I saw nothing of them,' says Séamaisín. 'I was asleep, I dare say.'

'You and everyone else in the village along with you,' says Tadhg. 'Each currach had over a thousand scad. They were west in Inis Tuaisceart overnight and if the tide had not come too early they would have caught enough of them for the whole Island.'

'Upon my soul, they're the men for you—their boats full of fish and other people still asleep!' says Séamaisín.

November 1919

Beach, Slea Head, Blaskets in the distance

Abundance without Profit

'THE Dunquin people brought their fish back from Dingle yesterday unsold,' says the Yank, 'and a great share of it came home further up the coast too. No one ever before saw as big a haul of fish as reached Dingle yesterday from every quarter.'

'I'm sure they could get no price for it, seeing that they all carted it there,' declares Séamaisín. 'My curse on them for buyers, what is to stop them giving a decent price always beyond what they offer.'

'Four shillings was the price at the start of the day and they wouldn't give a halfpenny for it after that because enough hands were not to be found to deal with it. There wasn't a man in the district idle and the same number again wouldn't be able to finish the job.'

'No currach came from Dunquin tonight fishing,' says Séamaisín, 'and I dare say they won't come, nor tomorrow either. If they had planned to salt a barrel or two for themselves, the salt is too dear for that as well—seven shillings a hundredweight, and it doesn't go too far at that.'

'They have enough of it salted at home already,' says the Yank, 'herring and every other class of fish, and I suppose it is no small matter to them to have the house full of relish.'

'They will be able to sleep their fill so,' says Séamaisín.

November 1919

Pulling the Tooth

'WHERE did you spend the day since morning?' Nell asks Tadhg.

'With the devil wisha, my dear woman, in a place where I was caught in a predicament if ever I was.'

'Mary, Holy Mother! What happened to you today? You weren't out in a boat or on the hill.'

'I would have been better off. I happened to call in to see that poor misfortune of a cripple east yonder, and he stuck in a corner for a month without life or health. I wanted to see how he was faring and, by Holy Mary, no one need ask. A glance at his face is enough. He has the look and signs of death on him.'

'If he has itself,' says Nell, 'isn't it often before you saw a man in that state and he didn't cause you such a fright.'

'Yerra, woman, didn't I often lay the dead in the coffin without fear or dread. This man wasn't dead but alive still, only with the look of death, and the man causing the fright standing there in front of him.'

'O Lord, who was that?'

'The Doctor that was in the village today, and what do you think but didn't the sick man see him passing the door. He told me to call him in. "Why?" says I. "I have a stump of a tooth that never left off plaguing me this past year and if I had it pulled out I might not feel so bad." I called the Doctor and straight in he came. He had no Irish, myself no English, nor had the sick man. We were three fools, each of us in the dark. In the heel of the hunt I conveyed to the gentleman that a bad tooth was the bother and that he wanted to be rid of it. Faith, the Doctor soon had the pincers in his hand and a grip on the back of the sick man's head.

'With that the look of the dying came over him, for he thought the Doctor would be the cause of his death there and then. He frightened the Doctor, who gave me the job of holding him while he made three attempts to draw the tooth before he succeeded. I'd swear a piece of the jawbone came with it. Blood spouted and he's at his last gasp. I won't get over it for the rest of the year.'

November 1919

A Hoax about English Wives for Pensioners!

'ANY news from the boats today?' one old age pensioner asks another.

'There was, boy!' says he. 'You'll have an extra half-crown every week from now on.'

'God help us,' says Pádraig, 'we have need of the increase.'

'But I don't think that half-crown will give any help from God or Mary to you,' answered Seán, 'or to anyone else either.'

'Isn't it as good for us as for other people?'

'Not a bit of it,' says Seán. 'So long as you, and myself along with you, will have to keep a lump of an Englishwoman from now on, and you'll have to marry her, and no thanks to you either.'

'Oyeh, wisha, the devil sweep her from me!' says Pádraig, 'what misfortune is sending them over? Are there many coming?'

'Four thousand widows,' Seán answers. 'The authorities want to charge them on Ireland. They are soldiers' wives, and pensioners will have to marry them.'

'I'd rather see them in Hell than marry any old article across from England. By Our Lady, if they were from Ireland itself I might have some feeling for them,' declares Pádraig.

'If you refuse the widow, you'll lose the pension.'

'Then let me lose it! I'd prefer beggary and to be contented,' says Pádraig.

December 1919

Matchmaking at Shrovetide[1]

EIBHLÍN and Cáit stroll in to me for a visit at the start of the night:

'A week of Shrovetide is gone, Cáit, and it seems a short Shrove this year.'

Cáit: Holy Mary! It is short. As for myself and Eibhlín here, with the weather so rough, I'm afraid it will pass us by.

Eibhlín: Bad scran to you, Cáit! If you have a wish to marry there's no call to drag me along in your wake.

Cáit: No need, on my oath wisha, Eibhlín. If there was any good match on offer, you're the one that would not let it come my way—small blame to you.

'Faith, she's as blunt as you are,' I put in.

Cáit: Upon my soul, she is! She has a head and body on her, boy, if any slip of a girl has, and I'm very much afraid she'll rob me of the best man.

Eibhlín: On my oath, if I were every bit as old as you are, maybe you wouldn't have anything to crow about.

Cáit: Aroo, little hussy, isn't it thinner I'm getting. When I was your age I was a stone heavier than I am today.

Eibhlín: May you be another stone lighter this time next year and you'll be the handsomer for it.

Cáit: May God not heed you! On my soul, my poor bones need the sleek covering they have on them now for the life that's in store for them.

---

[1] Here Shrovetide means the time for matchmaking between Christmas and Twelfth Night, the marriage to take place the following Shrove.

'Would it be any wonder if the pair of ye were on yeer way this year,' says I.

Cáit: On my soul, we will, or fail in the attempt.'

Shrovetide 1920

Shrovetide Gossip

WHERE the paths cross, north west of my house, people gather from this side and that, and they come down from the upper end of the village. The same crossing could be called the village fount of knowledge.

There is a good gathering there at the time when Diarmaid Bán comes up and joins us.

'Any news from the upper end of the village for us?' asks old Eoghan.

'No,' says he.

'Hasn't he news himself for you?' Tadhg the Joker butts in.

'What's that?' Eoghan asks.

'That he wouldn't let a wife in the door to his son, without a dowry of one hundred pounds.'

'Oh! Don't be putting a lie on my poor man,' says Eoghan.

'I'm putting no lie on him,' says Tadhg. 'I've heard it talked about for the past two days all over the village.'

'Is this true, Diarmaid?' asks old Eoghan.

'It is.'

'May that be the hundred that will never do you any good —not that I need to wish it on you—and may the span of his days be less than a hundred for any man who would make you a gift of it!'

Shrovetide 1920

News of a Match

NEWS of a match for Micheál Dhomhnaill has come from the mainland. Great excitement in the village. Some are going to the wedding.

I was visiting a house where there is a big family. There was no sorrier sight than the woman of the house trying to get them to do a stroke of work. Some of the men-folk were on the strand, gathering seaweed. Dinner time was approaching. The mother shouted:

'Brighde! Did you put the clothes out to dry yet?'

'Upon my soul I didn't, wisha!'

'Micí! Did you fetch the ass yet?'

'I didn't, wisha, upon my soul!'

'Máire! Have you the fire going yet?'

'I haven't, wisha, by my baptism!'

'Mary, Holy Mother, what scattered yeer senses for all of ye this day? I suppose what's driving ye out of yeer wits is this fuss over marriage in the village.'

She put her head out of the door and saw the men coming back from the strand.

'Brighde, aroo, look! the men are coming back from the strand. What way are the potatoes? Are they nearly boiled?'

'I've only just hung the pot over the fire,' answered Brighde.

''Tis your fault!' said the mother. 'Don't be in the house when your father gets here; but, sure, I stand in greater danger than yourself.'

Shrovetide 1920

'Did any Young Man come to offer for you yet?'

As I walked along the roadway I met a couple of strapping young women. One wore high boots and the other low shoes. On these splashes of mud landed now and again. One young woman had a head of curly black hair and the hair of the other was auburn.

'Your legs are spattered,' said I to the red-haired lass. 'Why is that?'

'I'm wearing dancing shoes. I had no idea the paths were so muddy.'

'What did they cost you?'

'A pound.'

'Have you any others?'

'I have some high boots.'

'What did they cost?'

'Two pounds.'

'That's three pounds you've spent on your feet,' said I. 'I dare say if I had to take you through the shop in Dingle, I would need twenty pounds to dress you up from crown to toe.'

'It would not be enough,' said she, 'for the day I was there I parted with fifteen pounds, and many articles I could have bought I wasn't looking for at all, since I had them already.'

'Did any young man come to offer for you yet?'

'Holy Mary! They did not. I am too young still.'

'But it is known that your father has the few pennies and a story like that travels fast enough. It's different when a man is without them.'

'But my father would have no money saved even if the mint were making it for him,' said she. 'There's a houseful of us there, God bless us, and the expense too heavy.'

I was aware by this time that she had had enough of me and

that she felt that the black-haired lass was getting off too lightly listening to us, for she suddenly burst out:

'It is her father that has the money! Signs on it, many the young man comes to the house to offer for her.'

'Is that true?' I asked the dark young woman.

'Oh! A couple of offers reached us, but we did not think they were very suitable and nothing came of it.'

'And the man who has not come forward yet, maybe, doesn't find ye suitable, so ye would have to bide yeer time for another year,' said I.

'Let him suit himself,' she answered.

I turned to the red-head:

'Compared to her mane, your head of hair shines like gold. But however much it may look like it, it seems you'd rather have some share of real gold in your hand.'

'Oh! "Isn't it money that showers blessings on the people altogether",' said she.

'Well, never ye mind, there is still time for a last fling left in Shrovetide. I suspect from my judgment of ye that the pair of ye will be snapped up. We have shortened the day, so good day to ye!'

'The same to you,' they replied.

Shrovetide 1920

The Cure

I WAS standing at the foot of the Long Field. Séamaisín and myself had come back from the strand. Down strides Séamas to us with a white rag tied round his chin.

'What's troubling you?' Séamaisín asks.

'Trouble enough, wisha, my darling man,' says he, 'every tooth in my head and it throbbing with pain and ache.'

'Are you looking for any cure for them?' Séamaisín asks.

'There's no cure they'd rather have, or that gives them more ease, than to be chewing a plug of tobacco.'

'And why don't you give them one?'

'I haven't got it, my dear man.'

'May you not have a tooth, good or bad, left in your gums this time tomorrow, if every tooth in your head is destroyed for want of a piece of tobacco for them to chew. You have only your own back to clothe and your own mouth to feed!' says Séamaisín.

'Well,' says Séamas, 'every one of your words is forgiven, if you have any piece I could give them to chew.'

'I have, wisha, and enough for your wake,[1] but I'd rather fling it into the wide sea than let you have any piece of it, you mean skinflint,' says Séamaisín.

I thought that answer strange and wondered which of the two was worse, the man seeking the cure or the man who had it and would not part with it.

'People cross each other's path but hills and mountains do not,' I reflected, and the day would come, maybe, when the man in pain could stretch a helping hand himself. I reflected also that the same God had sent the pain to one man and the cure to the other. I shoved my hand in my pocket and gave him a good

---

[1] Tobacco and clay pipes were distributed to the mourners.

chunk of tobacco. He seized it while he called down blessings on me, saying:

'May you have all the share of luck meant for those travelling the road for a year!'

Everyone there wondered at him, and a good number had gathered by this time.

The next day I was taken by surprise when he landed in the door with two shillings worth of tobacco for me and seven thousand blessings too. His toothache had vanished.

''Tis ever said, Séamas,' said I, 'that good never went astray on anyone.'

'May it not go astray on you in God's Paradise!' he replied.

January 1920

A Man with the Seven Cares of the
Mountain on his Shoulders

I WAS standing on the bank above my house. Seán Shéamais went by.

'Where are you hoisting sail for now, in God's name?' I asked.

'That's more than I can tell you, except I have the seven cares of the mountain on my shoulders, with no end of things to do, and I'm making a start on none of them.'

'It is often before now that a man pitched away his last and his awls when he had too much to face,' said I.

'I'm in the same case,' he answered. 'There are people gathering seaweed. I need turf. I have sheep to dip. I need flour. I have a wall to repair. I have a shed to rebuild. I have a trawl-line to see to and a net to prepare. I left the house now to have a day away from it all, for I couldn't decide which should be tackled first.'

As he is my brother's son, I did not want to see him wasting his time for lack of good advice to put a stop to it:

'Any man ever who has all his tasks staring him in the face must owe a good share of that to his own neglect,' said I. 'Don't ever follow the example of the man who is not ahead of his work with everything put safely behind him. Go home now and finish one of them, and then it won't be facing you tomorrow.'

February 1920

'Where did Ye Leave yeer Father?'

I MEET a couple of lads on the path.

'What's all the hurry on ye now?' I ask.

'Our father is on the strand and we're going to call him home.'

'Why?'

'To come to the table.'

'If it's tea ye have won't it keep for him?'

'No, man, 'tis potatoes, and they would go cold if he didn't come for them.'

'But if the sea is coming in on the seaweed, how can he come for the potatoes?'

'Oh, if the tide is sweeping the seaweed away he doesn't have to come. We'll come back home, and for him there will be tea.'

'Is it tea without sugar?'

'Holy Mary, what else! We had no sugar for ages and no colouring either, only a small tin of condensed milk now and again. Come on, Donncha, that fellow would keep us here till dark.'

'Be off with ye, I'll be strolling up and down here till ye come back, but ye won't have yeer father with ye, I fear.'

Away they ran like a pair of young hounds and I was not long pacing up and down before I saw them coming back.

'Where did ye leave yeer father?'

'He's where he has his hands full,' said one of them. 'A great heap of seaweed gathered and the tide coming in on him!'

'The tide will sweep yeer father away.'

'Keep an eye on him!' they cried.

February 1920

As the Ear Hears

I STAND a while gazing east and west. Four men are below at the harbour's edge, painting a currach. Two women with creels full of clothes on their shoulders are going to the cliff well to wash them. There is a second currach afloat searching for salvage around Beiginis. Other people with a drove of asses are going out along the road to fetch turf. Others again have cows round the house still, waiting to be driven onto the hill.

A woman puts her head out of the door and sees the cow, her calf and the ass. She shouts at the top of her voice for Siobhán. No answer. A lad of hers comes up.

'Where's Siobhán, Micheál?'

'She's on the White Strand.'

'The Devil fetch her up from there! Drive them up to pasture yourself.'

'I will not, wisha, upon my soul. I'm late for school as it is.'

'Where's Peig so?'

'I don't know where she is.'

'Mary, Holy Mother! They'll be round the house till night-fall. And what matter to me, only that yeer father is on the mainland. Drive them on up for me and let them have their head,' says she.

Another woman sticks her head out.

'Go to the strand and fetch a grain of sand for me. Isn't this house drowned wet after the day's washing,' says she to one of her children called Brighde.

'Why should I, wisha, upon my soul! And there's Nora hopping and skipping from cabin to cabin for herself and not a stroke done by her since morning.'

I wander on to the upper end of the village, and the next voice I hear is the King's. Since he is a fine figure of a man, powerful and strong, he had a voice to match directing the cow, the ass and the dog. And since he has the use of two languages, no two commands together were in the same one. You would think the animals understood his English better than his Irish!

I look up towards the Holy Well and see as many women gathered there as there are in Killarney, or so you would think. Many have buckets, bowls, kettles for water; others have twin-handled tubs full of clothes to wash, and on top of each tub, soap and a beetle for beating the clothes. Steam coming out of the mouth of every woman with the dint of work. I doubt whether any other patch of ground in Ireland would have beaten this one for chatter at that moment. They drowned the noise of the King and the noise of the ocean too and, although I was not too far away from them at the time and they were speaking Irish, I understood their chatter no more than if they had come from France.

Beginning of Spring 1920

The Great Blasket

And as the Eye Beholds

I TURNED east towards the road. I looked up towards the village well and it was a marvel to behold. Women, children and toddlers—there they all were. Some of the children were dipping their heads in the water, washing their faces for school. One doused his head and when he rose had the towel ready to dry it, with the rest to the end of the line following suit. Off with them down towards the schoolhouse. The mother of each, without stirring hand or foot, let them see to themselves.

An outcrop of rock stands a little way from the well and all the grown men who could squeeze in had their backs against it, while they waited for others, who were not ready yet, to join the company. They were arguing fine points of every law under the sun and, although half of them did not know A from B, they aired as much knowledge of the laws as Aristotle.[1]

When they were all gathered they took to the road, driving about thirty asses in front of them. If one or two had a feeble croak, others could be heard three miles from home. You could not miss the booming voices of the King and Tadhg, however loud the rest.

Beginning of spring 1920

[1] The Islanders told stories about Aristotle. They believed he was a wise man with three sons who left home in turn to seek their fortunes.

Sun of Brightness and Youth

THE sun was high when I wandered out. The way the day had
cleared would make you reflect that it was not the end of the
world yet, maybe. New grass was sprouting like a living crea-
ture, as if invited by the radiance of the sun to rise out of its sleep.
The grim aspect had vanished from mountains and hills by this
time and they wore a look of gaiety and joy, for the sunshine that
had come now had the power to bring swift change. The sky had
not cleared like this since All Hallowtide. It banished the mist
and dreariness everywhere and gave a lift to the heart and
health of the sinner too.

There was also a change over the wide sea, although this was
not so marked, for the wild sea rages too high and the sunshine
does not restore it to calm so quickly. The change was great,
though white foam was spraying on all sides and the sea seemed
fearful of another battering from the skies. It was far from
having its own natural colour yet and did not look too settled.

I was strolling along in this fashion observing everything
until the coasts came in sight. There another wonder struck me:
the damage caused by the great storm. There is no doubt that
the works of man are wonderful and what he has accomplished
all over the world, but look at what the great sea has done with
the power of God and it will make you ponder awhile. The
pillars of rock uprooted by the sea, the islets wrenched out of
their foundations, the big islands stripped of their topsoil along
with the grass, the rocks swept from one end of the shore to
the other, many gone altogether. There are those who would
scarcely believe you that any power exists surpassing what they
can see with their own two eyes. Foolishness!

Beginning of spring 1920

A Fine Day in March

THE day that looked most like summer since All Hallowtide. This being so, I was impatient to be ready for a walk round my native place. I set out and strolled along. A currach was approaching the harbour at this time with some salvage. Many signs were visible to me now that had been hidden by the winter. The little birds were skimming the waves, each with his own tune. Anyone would swear they were a small shoal of people just let out from a college of music. The usual fish of the sea—the fish always there during their season—were venturing to raise their heads out of the water from time to time, so that you would imagine they were greeting one another. Indeed who dare say otherwise? Is not the same Master over them and ourselves?

I strolled further along, gazing at patches of every hue on the ocean, something that would mystify those too young to have any sense yet. It is otherwise with me, however: my teeth have worn away during the time I have been looking at such sights. What is the cause of the colours? The small clouds above in the sky, each able to cast its own hue and shade on the great sea.

March 1920

The King's Speech

SOME men were standing round the King. He had dug a good piece of ground but his courage had failed him for sowing any seed there. The reason: the change for the worse in the weather. He made a speech, and many had gathered by now.

He declared that he was sixty-five years old himself and he had never seen nor heard of any year like it. There was snow, and rot in the ground. It was no use sowing seed there for, even if it sprouted, it would wilt afterwards and there would be no crop. Moreover—there was strife in the great world and there was no knowing when it would end. It was no use trying to do a stroke when life was in such confusion.

There were some there at the time who had never before heard a speech from the King. They thought he must have heard a voice from Heaven revealing all this to him and they began to shiver with dread, until they found out otherwise.

A man spoke up saying that the seed is sown every year and no one ever knows the outcome: they simply put their trust in God. Maybe this year would turn out well yet.

March 1920

Chat

TODAY I have finished the work on what potatoes I have planted around the house, where I have them this year, until I find an opportunity to go to the Field of the White Strand. I am impatient for the day, since no matter what bad health is threatening me, it vanishes quickly when I am working in that field.

Between times, I headed towards the untilled field below the new houses[1] to mend and strengthen a wall there, while I had little else to do. But it is not a road that is short of chat: the Lord Mayor of Cork is dead;[2] Ireland's envoy in America[3] has only to make one more speech and the crown of Ireland will be placed on his head; Carson's own men were leaving him in the lurch; the English leaders were coming to blows with one another over Ireland; the grand, broad harbour of Ventry had been surveyed for a short cut by American ships. In the upshot I came home to dinner without putting so much as one sod, or stone either, on the wall.

The King calls round to my house on his way back from the field to ask me where Tadhg the Joker was; he had been lonesome after him since morning. 'But,' says he, 'he has lost his senses this year where work is concerned. He has been poor company.'

'But he says it is you that have lost yours!' I answered.

*   *   *

[1] Five slate-roofed two-storeyed houses, built by the Congested Districts Board in 1910. The older houses were single-storeyed and roofed with tarred felt.

[2] Thomas MacCurtain, shot dead by Crown Forces on 20 March 1920.

[3] Éamonn de Valera.

I happened to meet Donncha. After chatting for a while about the ways of the world, he said:

'You never attend the parliament house we have here in the village.'

'I do not. Ye have no great rules there, I fear.'

'Oh, certainly not in that house, for we are not of one voice, and I dare say before long it will lead to bloodshed between us.'

'Diarmaid's is yeer debating chamber.'

'It is, and the house is packed every night, every man voicing his own opinion.'

'Are ye debating this matter there?'

'What matter is that?'

'That the flag of Ireland is overstamped now on letters coming from America, whereas it is not long since the censor's knife[1] was being applied to letters that had no flag on them.'

'That matter came up for discussion,' says Donncha, 'but no one would believe it and when I argued with them that it was true, it nearly was the end of me.'

'If I had known, it was easy for me to rescue you.'

'Holy Mary! How?'

'Because I have a letter with the flag of Ireland on it.'

'Mary, Holy Mother! Wasn't it a pity I did not know that last night.'

'Won't tonight do?'

'I'll send a youngster down for it this evening,' said Donncha.

'But maybe they won't thank you for it.'

'I don't care in the devil!' he said.

Spring 1920

---

[1] During the Great War.

Séamaisín's Potato Sets

WE were standing where the paths cross near the houses —Dónall, the Yank, old Eoghan, Tadhg the Joker and many more of us—chatting about the ways of the world. Who should come along but Séamaisín, a bag across his back with a handful of Blacks to sow.[1] Anyone who did not know him would swear that he had been a beggarman ever since he left the cradle. The figure he cut brought a smile they could not repress to everyone's lips. Dear as clothes are at present, no one there would have given sixpence for what he had covering his bones.

No one could muster enough courage to speak to him but, since he is Séamas' uncle, he greeted him.

'God save you, uncle!' said he.

'The same God save you,' the uncle replied.

'Is it potato sets you have there?'

'It is.'

'Isn't it great courage you have and to be planting them in this class of weather,' said Séamas.

'Didn't you have greater courage still yesterday and to head for the open sea from Dunquin, when you knew about the bad weather from seeing it with your own two eyes. I cannot tell what God will do with these, and all we could ever do was put our trust in Him,' was Séamaisín's reply.

'Look at these men here that wouldn't plant a potato and they split ready,' said Séamas.

'Oh! these, I dare say, are saintly men and 'tis how He told them not to sow, that there would be no crop; but maybe too they are mistaken,' Séamaisín said.

Spring 1920

---

[1] A strain of potatoes.

Every Train in Ireland Halted

TODAY the people of the Island are filled with fear. A currach has come in with the news that every train in Ireland was halted. There was no bite of food to be found; this and that had happened; men in gaol were dying on hunger-strike; the world was upside down; no pig or bullock would be allowed to leave the country from now on; no one knew what crime the men being put to death in gaol had committed; fighting would soon break out.[1]

When I tired of listening to all this I walked on along the path. Other men strolled by, since they had no inclination for work, as would be usual with them at this time of the year. I happened to meet Séamaisín.

'Did you hear the news?'

'What news, Séamaisín?'

'Didn't you hear the stories that are flying round the village?'

'I did, Séamaisín.'

'The world has gone to rack and ruin!' said he.

End of spring 1920

---

[1] Anglo-Irish War, January 1919 to July 1921.

Cliff Danger

I WAS gathering a handful of mussels to manure the field for an early crop of potatoes. I had only a small bag gathered east towards the harbour when my son, Seán, came up to call me home. I couldn't make it out.

He called me again and again.

'Why?' I asked.

'Peig Sayers's son Tomás[1] has fallen down a cliff,' he said.

His news drove away whatever wish I had for gathering mussels and I turned for home. I put away what I had gathered and when I reached the house I was able to find out exactly what had happened. Five of them—big strapping lads from the upper village—had been gathering furze for fuel on the north side of the hill in a bad place. This lad was pulling a tuft. He toppled over taking the tuft with him, save us and guard us! Down with him until he struck the water. He was lifted out by a currach. There was a wake over him for two nights. He was buried in Ventry. God rest his soul!—the young man, the best Gaelic scholar on the Island, especially for reading the language.

There was silence in our house as the sorrow was too great over the way he died.[2]

May 1920

---

[1] Aged twenty-one. His brother Micheál O'Guiheen 'The Poet' wrote a long lament for him.

[2] A son of Tomás himself, aged seven or eight, fell over a cliff and was drowned about the year 1890.

In the Field of the White Strand

I WAS working in the Field of the White Strand. A delightful day. There has been little sign of summer this year until now. The mountains were aglow with every hue. A fire was burning here and there, tokens that people were cutting turf in various parts of the bog. The sea was calm with currachs coming and going. Seán Léan was rowing a currach, all by himself, as proud as the Prince of Wales in his stately yacht. The fish were lifting their heads out of the water, the birds singing their music and on land the people were stripped to their shirts, re-earthing the potatoes. Groups were coming down both sides of the hill with bundles of furze and children raced east along the slope after morning school. Smoke was rising from every house at this time—dinner on the way surely.

May 1920

The Hoaxer

'MARY, Holy Mother!' exclaims a woman above in the middle of the village. 'How is it the spray is not doing the potatoes any good this year, compared with other years?'

'That's because the ground will not be giving any crop for three years,' says a man who was filling a can at the well to mix the spray.

'O Lord! Who knows that, only God. If it takes so long, the ground might as well not be there at all, for there won't be anyone left alive on it.'

The hoaxer spoke up again saying that maybe there is plenty of room in Paradise and what a pity it would be not to fill it up, rather than to have the miserable hungry life we have of it here.

'Upon my soul, whatever roast meat they have up there, not many here would wish to join them,' said she.

'They will change their minds,' he said, 'when they have spent three days or a week without a bite to eat.'

He picked up his can of water and left us there.

'Swopping chat with women won't spray the potatoes,' said he.

'Isn't he the smart boyo?' said I.

'He can't escape what's in his blood,' she answered. 'There was no greater hoaxer in Ireland than his own father.'

June 1920

The Women at the Well

Up and down the main road I went with an ass drawing turf for the fire, though this year there is not much to be said for it as fuel. However, it would be a great help to me, I thought, if I managed to draw the winter's fuel down from the hill. There is a well on my way up and the name I have for it myself is the Holy Well; most christen it the Yank's Well. I don't suppose there is another well in Ireland where so many women gather round during the day. The man who compared them to geese had the right word for them.

I arrived at the Holy Well. If there were not women gathered round it, it is not day yet. There were at least a score there with their buckets, and it was not waiting for water that delayed them, but whiling away the day together having a gossip. Potatoes and turf they were discussing and, at this hour of the day and from the spate of talk, you would think that it was from the heavens they had descended with some revelation from Paradise.

'Did ye pick the new potatoes yet?' one woman asked another.

'We did.'

'Were they any good?'

'They were not. "Even lard has a right to its name", so I must call this season's crop "potatoes". They were not fit for hen or pig or dog. They were not fit for food, seed or market, and they were small, black and sparse into the bargain.'

'Nobody could have summed them up better.'

'There never was any crop of potatoes any year the fish shoal among them,' said another.

Every patch of blight to be seen in all the fields at this time looked like a shoal of fish, and wasn't she the sharp woman to make the comparison.

'Any year you see the black pigs and the white pigs in the

sky together, it will make a year without fuel,' said someone else.

And so they went on.

Although it is hard to fault God's gift, praise be to Him for ever—and this well was a great boon in the middle of the village whenever water was scarce—see how the day is being frittered away around it and chores put back as a result. There were three men there who would have had their buckets full of water in the time they spent listening to the chatter of these women, and I myself would have had my load of turf well clamped in the time I was there.

I suppose if six of the best of these women were in Dáil Éireann[1] it would not prove so hard to make the laws of the country as it is.

June 1920

[1] Irish Parliament.

Boy on the northern side of the Great Blasket. In the rear is the road to Gravel Strand and the island of Beiginis

The Woman Footing[1] Turf

IT was a grand day. Young and old—each with his own task—footing the turf, piling it into windrows, clamping it into a rick and much of it being brought home. On my way up the hill to draw a load with the ass, I met Máire, a hearty strong woman. She was footing turf and singing a song; it came slow and soft and sweet and could be heard far off.

'God save you, Máire.'

'God and Mary save you.'

'The day isn't coming hard on you, God bless you, and you to be singing that grand burst of song.'

'When I'm working hard, that's when I prefer to sing a couple of bars. When the voice weakens on me I feel the work weakening on me too.'

'Are you fasting since morning?'

'I'm not, on my oath!' said she. 'I brought a fine hunk of bread with me and I have swallowed it back since morning.'

''Tis ever said, Máire, that "food is the workhorse".'

'By my baptism, you can be sure of it! But for chewing that wedge of a loaf since morning, I would be laid out beside that clump of grass there in front of you.'

'Maybe the good drying weather is on its way, Máire.'

'Maybe so, with God's help! It would be a great ease for poor people to have the fire. It's enough for them to be worried about the food.'

'Fire, food and clothes are the three needs that bring all the drudgery, Máire.'

'By my baptism, you can be sure and certain of it,' she said.

July 1920

---

[1] Setting it on end in small heaps to dry.

Confusion

ALL the fishermen were gathered together to go out, but a dispute arose over the boats. Feidhlim, a pensioner, had a son in America, whose share of one boat was being taken over by the other two partners. They however had no intention of compensating Feidhlim for it. Battle was on because Feidhlim had no intention either of letting them take the boat without paying up. One of the pair taking it out was a son of Tadhg the Joker. The two old men, Tadhg and Feidhlim, let fly at one another with the tongue and there was nothing they left unsaid. However, Feidhlim prevented the currach going out that night.

There is a big lump on the nape of Feidhlim's neck and Tadhg flung at him that it was full of roguery and this roguery of his was making it swell; 'but his own self to the devil! if he had a knife, it would swell no more on him for he would lance it himself.'

Feidhlim was beside himself with rage. He flung off his waistcoat and thrust his fist up against the other fellow's face. The men there came between and parted them.

Then Feidhlim declared that no scoundrel ever lived that he wouldn't scatter his tripes on the ground for him!

They had a lively day of it.

July 1920

Old Mící

'Isn't it a great day for gannets today,' says old Mící—with his walking stick and goatee beard—as he gazed up at the clouds, casting a glance every now and then at the wide sea. From the figure he cut any man who did not know him would swear he was an old admiral of the sea, retired after serving his term.

'The things people think of when they've nothing to do!' a woman tosses at him as she strides by.

September 1920

Currachs Fishing

THIS evening I was returning home from the Field of the White Strand in no great hurry, for the weather was splendid. It put me in mind of the grand gentlemen who often accompanied me on such an evening.[1]

When I thought of them I stopped and gazed all around me. The sinking sun was glowing yellow at this time for it was beginning to slide into the shade of the horizon for us, hurrying along with the same momentum that would bring its rise in due time for the rest of the human race.

Between me and Dunquin a dozen currachs were heading for the night's fishing on the Blasket bank. About the same number were leaving the Island harbour. I rested on my heels a good while, in no great hurry, until the two clans reached the same fishing ground north of Beiginis. It is often a man beheld a worse sight than twenty-four currachs afloat in the same fishing ground in the open sea, waiting for nightfall to pay out their nets in the water, hoping for God's gift.

I walked on another stretch of the path, making straight for the house until I reached the strand road. As I turned down I saw as many as twenty women, young and old, coming up together, each carrying her own bag of sand on her back.[2]

October 1920

---

[1] Learning Irish from Tomás.
[2] Put down to dry the floors of the houses.

'Death Has his Eye on Me!'

LIVING on his own in the village there is a man they call Big Tomás. There has been no one in the house with him for a long while. A man like him goes on well enough until sickness or trouble strikes. Then he is not to be envied, and so it was in this case.

Some of the lads called in to him the other day. It is in the company of such a man that they prefer to pass the time, because in a house like his everything is at sixes and sevens. This day, several had gathered in, amusing themselves as usual.

They were not there long before they heard the squawking of a goose.

'Do ye hear the goose?' asked one. 'Or wherever in the house is she?'

The search was on, and the very lads there to carry it out, but despite all their searching no goose was to be found. When they left off ransacking the place, the goose was squawking away triumphantly still. There was no one in the house but was puzzled and completely baffled: the middle of the day, several people there, a goose cackling away in their midst and no notion where she was.

The squawking of the goose was growing louder day by day and when everyone learned that it could be heard day and night, it caused great wonder. It was not long before the old women declared that something was going to happen, something bad by the look of it. They told their families to stay clear of the house—the goose was there for a purpose. This they did and the house was left to Tomás himself.

Big Tomás, the poor man, was not too happy either, but he was unwilling to abandon the house. The time the goose really went wild was when he was cooking his food over the fire. The old women had the explanation for that—it was to put him off eating!

Now, poor Tomás took to his bed and stayed there on the flat of his back. The next day his door was shut. Some people said that perhaps he was dead. No one went near him that day, until the same time the day after. Then a couple of lads moved up to the door and gave it a kick. Tomás answered.

'What's the matter with you?' they asked.

'There is little the matter with me,' said he.

'But what's keeping you in bed?'

'Oh, I have thrown in my hand. Death has his eye on me! For two days the gég-gég-gég has never weakened.'

The pair could hear it at this time too, but could not discover where it was coming from.

When they were leaving him they said his days were numbered; Death it was and he had come for the man of the house, no one else. Poor Tomás was in a sorry state when they left him; he was suffering from no ache or pain, only despair—a terrible affliction. A report that he was dying was what the pair brought home with them.

Very late that day a couple of lads went up to the chimney and peered down. What was below there but the goose and she was well singed. They told Tomás the goose was in the chimney. He hopped out of bed. They fetched a line and hook and hauled the goose up; she was as black as soot. She belonged to the schoolmaster and the ones that found her put her there, I'm thinking. Be that as it may, Tomás was next door to eternity by then without priest or monk.

He is up and about now and making a remarkable recovery.

October 1920

Life is Strangely Altered

THERE is a white mist over the mountains and round-topped hills. The sea is calm without boat or ship fishing in it. Life is strangely altered. There is no buyer standing around as was usual, waiting to see when a boat might come in with a handful of fish for him. The man who once saw the scene with the boats and the fish would find it an unfamiliar world now and be sorrow-stricken. When the news arrives in the papers about the state of Ireland at the present day, everything turned upside down without head or tail to it, you would notice some eyes shedding a fine soft tear and, alas, with good reason. The people have nothing coming in; all they had to depend on always was the living they could make by their own health and strength, and that is denied them now. There is nothing for them to do but lean their backs against the field walls. May God grant a better fate for every poor wretch! We will soon be going hungry unless He opens the gap.

October 1920

Tadhg is Given a Fright

TADHG the Joker called in to me with a story about the new room with a felt roof that he had built onto his residence—how his two sons kept getting such a fright while lying in bed there that they were on the point of abandoning it.

'Your own son was in the house with us around midday today and the racket there had us nearly falling over one another to get out of the house,' said Tahdg.

It is long since I laughed so heartily as I did at this and he thought I was laughing at him, but it wasn't so.

While they were being given such a fright in Tadhg's house I was in the potato plot nearby. I saw a grey crow on the roof and it was cawing Vrauk! Vrauk! Vrauk! Before long I saw my own big black dog jumping up onto the roof of the room. It was very slippery and it gave him all he could do to reach the joining with the house. The grey crow did not stir from its perch. The dog gave a single bound up to reach it, but it was too much for him. He tumbled all in a heap, crashing onto the house and from there to the ground.

That was the cause of the panic in Tadhg's household!

November 1920

The Storm

THE worst day of storm since the Famine years. A gale of exceptional fury, thunder and floods of rainwater. The deluge did not spare glen or bridge from its pounding. It swept out into the wide ocean anything that had stood more than seven years. The sea had turned yellow almost as far as Dunquin. The flood ran into many of the houses but there was no way of stopping it; they could only let it flow out the other side.

When there was a lull, the old people said the storm was not to be wondered at, for God was looking down on the great storms among the human race. Some of them said too that such storms among the people were always matched by a threat of the same from the skies.

The tempest is high and the sea raging, a high swell and a stormy sky, with every sign that it would not be today or tomorrow it would weary of its terrifying course.

'Mary, Holy Mother!' said one old woman. 'Will no fine day come this year? By the looks of this evening there will soon be blue mould coming on my pipe for lack of any shred of tobacco to put in it.'

'Isn't it all equal to you so long as you haven't blue mould in your belly for lack of food,' said I.

'I feel the want of tobacco more!' was the answer she made me.

December 1920

Tadhg Trapped

I HEARD the cross-talk flying thick and fast in the kitchen—it sounded like French, and yet they were speaking Irish, which is not a rapid language if it is spoken properly; but it was being mangled altogether this time by those gabbling it, whoever they were. I did not know as yet. Whatever I was writing, they were beginning to put me astray. A great rush of talk had come on them after the work of the day.

Soon I heard a fresh roar joining in. Who had arrived but Tadhg the Joker. He flung himself into the argument with the company that was there already. At that point I had to throw the pen down. I would have been driven to it if I had been half a mile away, let alone being in the same house.

I went down to the kitchen where I found a couple of Yanks with two other women from the village, and Tadhg in the middle of them. Tadhg was up against the four and he was no match for them until I came in.

'You're no match for the women, Tadhg!' said I.

'The devil himself wouldn't be a match for them,' he exclaimed, 'and faith that's no wonder—a couple of women home from America and another couple just as bad from the village here.'

'But, sure, if you would only fall in with what they are saying, you wouldn't be in any trouble.'

'The devil take them, wisha, I will not,' said he.

'But what's the cause of the battle between ye, Tadhg, if you don't mind my asking?'

'I don't mind, by my baptism, for you'll have to take my side against this pack of women.'

'Tell me what yeer argument is about,' said I.

'It is this,' said he. 'The fine good-looking girl that was in the village last year—these here say she wasn't good-looking at all;

only this girl and that is good-looking, when not one of them is three feet tall. What would you say?'

'You can't call a small woman good-looking.'

'But you can call her an attractive woman, if that's what she is.'

'You can't use the word "good-looking" for a thin skinny article either,' said one of the women. 'She would have to be buxom for a start. If she is fresh-faced into the bargain, you have a good-looking, attractive girl.'

'The small woman is dumpy, a "*pantalóg*"; the thin skinny one is a scrag, a "*scáthainne*",' said I.

'The devil mend ye!' said Tadhg.

December 1920

Women's Gabble

My wonder grew while I sat in the room writing away. Little would I write as long as I live if there were four women there, their jawbones working, and nothing between me and them but the leaf of the door. One Yank was there from the start and a second came in, along with two other women. When the four set to and put the jawbones to work, I do not know what to compare them with, and although they have been compared to geese, no four geese since the time of Moses would outdo them for gabble.

Three hours they spent at it and the oddest thing to me was that whenever one of them was telling a humorous story she could scarcely speak for laughing. 'Never heed the man who will keep the fun of his tale to himself,' they used to say in the old days. They thought little of the person who would laugh at his own tale, at any rate until the others knew what there was to laugh at.

They had only just gone home when Tadhg the Joker strolled in.

'Oh, you missed the sport, Tadhg. A pity you weren't here before the women left.'

'Thanks be to God I was not!' said he.   *December 1920*

Rabbits, Seals and Seaweed

ANOTHER day fine with everyone going about his business. Two currachs went west to the small islands hunting. It was eight o'clock at night when they returned home. There was a five-man crew in each currach and every member of it had a dozen fat rabbits. They would have had more but for going hunting for seals in their usual cave haunts, because a gallon of lamp-oil costs three shillings and these seals are full of lamp-oil; all you have to do is render them down. There was no seal in any cave, where there had been so many all the year before that they were at one another's throats. But, like everything else, they have their own season. 'It's not every day Dónall Buí is marrying or can make the arrangements,' was the men's comment.

'Have you any seaweed today?' I questioned Séamaisín who had just driven his ass up from the strands, for it is there he spends his day at this time of the year.

'Oh! don't mention seaweed,' he replied. 'Bad luck to it, what weed there was went down the Sound south on the great swell.'

'May that be all we lose!' I said.

'Oh! life is fine and easy for you. Wasn't that weed choice for gathering,' he said.

January 1921

Blasket children

The Merchant Ship

TODAY has the look of summer, although it has been raining heavily for a week and all through the year, but there is no cold and the grass is growing as it should. I happened to put my head out of the door and saw sailing from the north, appearing from behind Fiach an Fhirtéaraigh, the finest merchant ship I ever beheld, and the biggest. Everyone said she was from America, and maybe she was too. She sailed the Sound south. There were three miles between her and another which would be thought a fine vessel but for the one ahead. As the sun was strong at this midday hour and the ships were splendid, you would think that if anyone in middling health spent a while on board one of them, he would feel a different man returning home.

Currachs are hauling supplies as fast as they can from Dunquin, for the sea is smooth and the breakers are stilled. People are depending on shop food three times a day, for most of them have had no potato since Christmas. Dogfish does not fetch a shilling a pound in London now, as it did during the war. You would know that, because no one is fishing for it and the fisherman has empty pockets. A thin time indeed it is for the man of the sea, however it may be for the man on land.

January 1921

A Funeral

A Good neighbour is dead in the Island today. 'Cuainí' was the name he went by. It was many the fish he caught. He was sixty years of age. The blessing of grace be on his soul.

The wind is rising this evening and it is bitterly cold, but I am snug inside the four walls of the house.

*   *   *

Today, the day of the funeral, the weather is fine. A great boon this for people living on islands because it is no easy matter to bury a man in his family graveyard if there is bad weather.[1]

Currachs from the mainland arrived last night and others came in today for the funeral. There were many currachs in the procession and they are a sight to behold at a time of favourable weather. If they have a fair wind the sails will be hoisted. There will be only three men in the boat with the corpse. A fourth man would not have room to ply the oars on account of the coffin.

At a funeral that came from Inishvickillaun a few years ago, on a fine summer's day, there were sixteen currachs. These cut through the water in single file. I never saw so many at any other funeral. I thought that day I never saw a sight so grand at sea. I was in one of the currachs myself, of course. It was a year when lobsters were being caught, and men from Iveragh were fishing off Inishvickillaun. It was they that conveyed the corpse eastwards; they played their part well.

May all those who are parted from us be in a better place than this, ourselves too when the time comes. Amen.

January 1921

---

[1] The Islanders were buried on the mainland, except for babies and drowned sailors, who were buried in the small Island graveyard.

The Wake

THE wake—Tadhg the Joker's account of the night. They had two horse-drawn carts in Dingle. In the first that reached the harbour for the Island there was a barrel of porter, and a half dozen bottles of whiskey too. At the start of the night a generous measure of the porter was handed round. Later on there was bread and tea and jam in plenty. Those with a fondness for drink had no interest whatever in the food. Drink, not food, was what suited them, for parching thirst was their trouble, not hunger. Accordingly, they made for the corner where the barrel of porter was set up and turned their backs on the part of the kitchen where the table was laid out. Four pints were poured for every man that round.

Tadhg went out in the course of the night and made for his own house, intending to break up the night and return to the wake-house for another space before morning. He had not been home long when he heard men coming. Eight of them there were—some of the crowd that had gathered round the barrel, seemingly. A meal was soon prepared for them, and they were the men to do justice to it. They had barely risen from the table when the rest, who were in from the mainland, arrived, and they sat down to the table too, of course.

'But my curse on them,' said Tadhg, 'not that I begrudge them what they ate, but they had me wandering about all night!'

January 1921

News From the Mainland

THERE are fires blazing on every hill over on the mainland. They are seldom seen except at turf-cutting time. But it is not turf that is uppermost in people's minds at the present time. Séamas spends all his day on the hill with the stock and he said he had grave misgivings about three warships he had seen going eastwards along Dingle Bay at full steam. Everyone had his own opinion then as to what the fires on the hills and the warships signified. We will have to wait for news from the mainland, though the stories from there have often turned out to be unfounded too. The Dingle train is stopped again. That was the news that came in.

'Wisha, she is often so,' says Séamaisín. 'They should have pitched her down some glen the first day ever. But, by Our Lady, Iveragh, or the city of Limerick, is not far away. Boats from here often travelled there before now.'

'Maybe Spiller's boat will stop in the Sound with flour for us,' says Séamas.

'If you have enough money to pay for it,' says Séamaisín.

February 1921

A Lovely and Delightful Day

A LOVELY and delightful day. The sun shone clear and bright. Judging by its face and aspect, the end of the world was nowhere near yet. As for dark or sullen looks, it had no trace of them, thanks be to God. The sea was a plain like level grassland, the hills and mountains unclouded, a transformation on everything your eye would rest on, the blessed planet covering all with beauty.

Now, when the horses of Ireland have begun working and ploughing—and it is the time of year for them—no one on the Blasket has put a hand to any work for the new season yet; they simply do not know which task they should undertake first. The sea gives them the best help to make a living, but so far they are being given no encouragement to catch lobster or crab, nor is it likely they will be.

They have a grand day for gathering furze. You would think most of the people of the Island had joined in the procession when you saw them there all coming down the hill, each carrying his own bundle. Fetching furze from the hill and goods from the mainland—these are the special tasks they are busy with still, though some have bought withes for making lobster pots, taking a chance that there will be a demand for lobsters this year yet. Putting the gear together is a great expense.

St. Gobnait's Day, 11 February 1921

Rust on the Spade

IT is another grand day. People have scattered east and west. A currach has gone to Dunquin. The postman went out to the mainland too, but he had no great load on the way back. He was none too pleased with events in the world outside. He had heard that America was turning against England. But flour was plentiful on the mainland and that pleased him, for he does not like scarcity.

A great number of rabbits have been brought back from the small islands, since the weather is very calm. Bright summer is what we have. I heard one man telling another today that it was the real summer, but the powers that be had failed to keep proper track of the seasons.

'When will you scrape the rust off your spade, Séamaisín?' a waggish lad asked him, for he is the small, rough-tongued, waspish Séamaisín and the youngsters make game of him.

'Won't it be soon enough for me to knock the rust off it when I have eaten up all my stock of potatoes,' said Séamaisín, 'but you, now—you should be bending your back to scrape it off by this time if you're to have the new potatoes early, for ye never had enough to last ye, and ye never will, seeing how neither the devil nor laziness would ever let ye look after them properly, once ye have planted them in the ground.'

'Isn't it in the care of the Sacred Lord everyone leaves them,' said the lively youth.

'Upon my soul,' said Séamaisín, 'but He is good to you if He manures the potatoes for you!'

February 1921

Gale from the North-West

TORRENTS of rain fell so heavily today that it nearly swept away the cows from the hill and the herdsman along with them. Tadhg the Joker was there, seeing to a new-born calf, and by the time they both arrived back at the house no one in Ireland would give thirty shillings for them. It is often Tadhg told a flimsy tale, but he had good grounds for this little story now, because it concerned himself.

'Upon my body and soul,' said he, 'if we had been caught up there at the mercy of the gale of wind that blew from the north-west after the downpour, herdsman, cow and sheep would have been swept away, never to be found again on the hill of this Island. I never credited that the sea was red anywhere in the world until today; but, by Our Lady, we have our own Red Sea today, the same as in the eastern world.'

'Holy Mary,' said Nell, 'what made it red this day beyond any other?'

'The same God who turned your skin yellow!' said Tadhg. 'Surely, you foolish woman, water never poured down like that since the days of the Ark!'

March 1921

Tadhg's Loaf

MARCH is causing us great hardship. It has broken out harsh, fierce and strong. For every two men who have some store, three have little left, maybe, and five have nothing at all. Furthermore there is no sign that there will be any change in the weather for making a run out even to Dunquin, where some provisions might be found.

Late in the evening there was a fine appetizing loaf of bread baked ready to lay on the table in Tadhg the Joker's house, but when he walked in the door after coming from the hill he saw this fine loaf at the bottom of the house; he picked it up and gazed at it.

'Upon my soul, but you're the good neighbour to take away the hunger in the life that's in it,' said he, 'but by Holy Mary you're too hot yet, and I never liked hot bread, so I'll put you outside under the sky and wind for a while till supper time.'

He placed the loaf on the window-ledge outside to cool and came back into the kitchen.

Soon it was supper time and the women put a different loaf on the table. Tadhg told his wife to fetch in the other one he had found at the bottom of the house and put out to cool, but when she went outside, there was no sign of it and no one has laid an eye on it since.

'There's no sign of it,' said his wife.

'May you be struck blind!' said he, darting out to see, but there wasn't a crumb of it there.

'My curse follow it and the one who stole it!' he cried.

March 1921

A Fine Day in March

IT is a fine day in March and when a fine day like that comes at this time of the year it would remind you that the fine months will soon be returning. The sea-bird with his wings floating on the water, basking in the warmth of the sun; the birds on land singing away for themselves. They give the impression, one way and another, that there was an end to their struggle for food evermore; there would be no call for it.

They have good reason for taking their ease on such a day. They are very hard pressed to find food in the height of the bad weather. When the fine day comes they soon find enough to eat. Then they bask in the sun to make up for the bad spell, and it is that ease that makes them sleek.

Not a bag of seed potatoes has been sown in this Island yet. Our King here plants an acre of potatoes every year and that acre is sprouting grass still. The King will have to turn it all over himself with the spade, and draw a load of turf every day too. The turf is two and a half miles from home—that is five miles there and back. He is sixty-seven years of age, in full fettle still with no sign of weakening. He is the noble King, with the same regard for high and low, God bless him!

March 1921

'How are Things on the Mainland?'

A MARCH day it may be, but there is much to be said in its praise. Seven currachs have been out and they thought the day would never come, because they had forage neither for cow nor man, owing to the spell of bad weather. Séamas came up towards me to the cliff top, with a half-sack of flour on his back and every bead of sweat on his forehead was as big as a periwinkle. He still had to carry up another half-sack, as well as a half-sack of yellow meal and some grain.

'How are things on the mainland?' I asked him. 'Or are goods getting any cheaper?'

'They are not, my sweet man. Two pounds for this on my back here, thirty shillings for the yellow meal, seven shillings for the pack of grain, not to mention the other small items. I dare say there isn't another town in Ireland where they charge the prices they do in Dingle.'

'May God grant they don't grow sleek on it!' says Séamaisín. 'Nor anyone belonging to them! That was the bad name they had always in Dingle and may it stick to them for evermore!'

'But the trains are being halted and the roads are being trenched.[1] It won't be long before there will not be a scrap to be found there,' says another man.

'If so,' says Séamaisín, 'surely it is in our power to cut through the great sea, thanks be to God. We shall find a way—in spite of them all.'

The day before Good Friday, March 1921

[1] During the Anglo-Irish War, 1919–1921.

Good Friday Fare

'A man who drinks milk on Good Friday is greatly to blame,
A house without meat Easter Sunday suffers great shame.'

An old saying

As long as I can remember it would be a very poor day, were fare from the strand not gathered on this Friday. The first time I ventured out today I saw the current in this direction slackening in the Sound, letting it be known that its own power had slipped away this round, and that another tide would be following on swiftly, whose force would make itself felt—that is the flood tide.

It was just the right time for gathering strand fare for this day. I turned west as is my habit, and came to the Field of the White Strand—my spade is kept there always—and I looked back towards the houses. The paths were black with people, young and old. I found nothing odd in that, for I knew what they were about. They made straight ahead until they reached the outer strand left bare by the low tide. Everyone had an iron implement in one hand and in the other a can or some other kind of vessel.

I saw then that I myself was the most foolish one among them, although I did not want to admit that yet. I put one hand in my pocket. In there was my small handkerchief and in my other hand I held the spade, so I hurried off from the field and faced for the shore. Who should meet me but the Crown Prince of the Blasket; he was keeping up the tradition along with everyone else.

Good Friday, March 1921

Sunday Mass

IT was a morning of bright sun. Every young man was sprucing himself up for Mass, for fear that what happened last year, when there were thirteen Sundays in a row without any Mass, might happen again. Six currachs prepared to set off and you may lop the tip of the ear off me if the sea wasn't rough with churning waves as they crossed over, the people on the Island having little hope that they could make the journey back either this day or the next. But 'the higher the storm rages, the nearer is the help of God' as the saying goes, and it is a true saying. The weather cleared for a beautiful day, thanks be to God.

'It is true that every year is not the same,' declared Séamaisín.

'What reason have you for saying that?' asked a lively youth that was amongst the men. He meant to start the music, for Séamaisín is a man whose strings give out a tune the minute they're plucked.

'You should know the reason as well as myself, you good-for-nothing,' said Séamaisín. 'Isn't it a great gift that there are six currachs gone to God's Mass today compared with last year, when no boat ventured out any Sunday for three months. But it is idle for God or man to favour some of ye, ye would have it all forgotten in no time!'

Easter Sunday 1921

The Pension

THERE is a saying that God's help is between us and the door—that is, closer at hand than the door. So it is with March. In recent days many a man said the end of the world was near, but today no one says so. There is much besides that we pretend to know, when we are far from knowing it at all. It is the knowledge that comes to us from on high that we have to give way to at every turn.

Although March is not over yet, it resembles April, for it is a glorious day. The man who has not put his head outside for half the year is walking in the open fields. They tell themselves the worst is over now since March has nearly passed. These are elderly men that the pension has made soft, men who had work in them still—a good number of them—but who are sparing their strength to keep drawing this easy money if only they look after themselves. Were it not for that same pension a person would end up in the Poorhouse. It is the nearest law to God's laws on this earth.[1]

As soon as a fine morning comes along after the bad day, people forget that they had ever known a bad day. The same applies to everything. There is a man planting potatoes today who has not been outside his door since All Hallowtide. We happened to meet and I welcomed him out.

'I have come away from the house, but I still have to make it back there,' said he.

End of March 1921

---

[1] In 1909 old-age pensions of 1*s* to 5*s* were introduced for those over seventy whose weekly income did not exceed 12*s*.

Blasket group taken in 1934 when Maurice O'Sullivan (second from left) returned for a visit after he had published *Twenty Years A-Growing*

Spars of Driftwood

THE rain was clattering down in the morning as if the wide ocean were pouring down on top of us, but before the breakfast was eaten the wind had dropped. Off with the currachs rowing east and west over the sea, for in the preceding days there had been bits of wreckage afloat. After a while searching they returned home and all they had was a handful of spars scarcely fit for anything but the fire. Many were waiting for them above the landing place, each airing his own opinion—one man asserting that the currachs had no driftwood and another saying that he should be struck blind—there was wreckage in every currach, timber too, plenty of it.

'They have a small amount of timber,' pronounced another man, 'but it is not wreckage.'

'It is not, I suppose,' said Séamaisín, whose blood was up with vexation now, for he thought the other fellow was starting to scoff.

'And I suppose,' said Séamaisín again, 'you'll be telling me next it is furze they have, seeing how bad your eyesight is!'

'My eyesight is every bit as good as yours,' said the other man, 'and you can go to the devil, but they have no spars of driftwood.'

'Did they pick up anything?'

'They did, scantlings—bits of timber the ships pitch overboard when they are finished with them.'

'May you be pitched overboard yourself, and soon!' said Séamaisín.

End of March 1921

An End to Idleness

A Busy day on this Island, although through the rest of the year you would imagine that no one had a scrap of work to do. Their custom is to spend the winter sleeping and that leaves them with the seven cares of the mountain on their shoulders when the work starts in earnest. Each task is still facing them instead of being put safely behind them, and everything comes in a mighty rush.

Well, there is a spring tide running and the currachs of the village are afloat, two men in some and three in others. They have ropes and sickles to reap the black seaweed for manure. But the potatoes have not been planted yet and the seaweed cannot be spread until the seed potatoes are in the ground. So, one old woman is busy spreading seaweed and heaping up the ridge, while another is planting the seed potatoes.

You never saw anything like the fields! Men and women! Youngsters making their way downhill, each with his own bundle of furze on his shoulders, to put a crust on the cake of bread for the people working in the fields. Below them other youngsters leaving the schoolhouse, and they are not the ones with the least chatter after escaping from their cage, for that is what the schoolhouse is like for them.

The grand sunshine of these days is ideal for attending to every task. You would love to hear the old women lilting away in the fields for themselves. One of the old customs.

End of March 1921

People Scattered East and West

A TYPICAL March day—harsh and wild. North-easterly showers, heavy, bitterly cold. Thick flurries of snow coming down. The Islanders are toiling under it without stop. They are hard at work at this time. They need manure and turf, and some are still planting potatoes, others sowing oats. People have scattered east and west. Some have crossed by sea to Dingle, others to Dunquin.

A currach was fishing for bait for the trawl-line during the night. Once they had the bait they spent the day on the trawl-line, but by evening all they had was one ray! That trade is at an end until life changes.

Some Islanders have the lobster pots in the sea already. Great eagerness is gripping the rest. They are stretching ropes to straighten them first. They will have to tar them then and tie on cork floats. Stones will have to be put in the pot too to make it sink to the seabed, for it is there this gentleman, the lobster, spends his life.

If idleness was ever known among the Islanders, it is not this year. I asked Séamas about the zeal for work this year beyond any other I remember.

'You are foolish, and that is rare with you,' says he, 'but don't you know that "when she falls on hard times, the old woman has to bestir herself." We have nothing left, my sweet man, unless God sends any blessing on this year.'

End of March 1921

Fish being Pitched Down the Slip

I Took a walk eastwards to the harbour in the evening and a group of men had gathered there already. Dispirited and dejected they were, and it was clear that life is gone to rack and ruin when you can say that about them, for till now it had been a place full of zest and gaiety. Their nets were hanging there and not a man with enough heart to load them into his boat.

A currach went laden with mackerel to Dingle—they had to take them over the sea across the bay—and it is said that they pitched them down the slip. All they had in the bottom of the currach when they came back were bits of wreckage they had picked up on the way.

I moved over to Maitiú, a man who loves a chat. He is a fine big fellow, still in full vigour, for he is a 'lone bird' who, having no children, has their share of flesh on him as well as his own, and always will have. Many would be baffled by this phrase maybe, but a 'lone bird' is a man who never marries. Maitiú is one of those sluggards, though he has more of a stoop from work than the man with a family dependent on him.

'Look at the fish threshing around and no one going out to catch them,' said he.

'Couldn't we eat a good share of it ourselves, Maitiú.'

'There isn't a grain of salt in this village to put on an egg,' said Maitiú. 'It costs nine shillings the hundredweight and the fish would not pay for the salt.'

April 1921

During the Shower

ON days when some of us meet together, everyone voices his own opinion. There are those with something worthwhile to say and those who rattle on but say nothing. A number of us happened to congregate, when we were driven to take shelter in a glen by a shower blowing from the north-west, which looked likely to worsen.

'Holy Mary,' said Séamas, 'will the winter last forever? Isn't this the fierce battering we're getting from the north now!'

'Curse you and your foolishness! Anyone would think you were born today or yesterday,' said Séamaisín, who was huddled shoulder to shoulder with him, crouched down on his hunkers then as miserable as everyone else. 'Isn't it the wonder to you that you haven't summer every day in the year. I suppose if you were in God's Paradise and had the power, you would bestow summer every day on us here. But, more likely still, you would let fly at us with a fierce squall that would kill half of us off!'

Everyone in the glen burst out laughing and, though the shower was hard and heavy, we never noticed it passing, over the sport with the pair of them.

'You are not fit to talk to,' said Séamas, 'and it isn't to you anyone is talking either.'

'The harsh weather of Cuckoo Time is ahead of you yet, maybe, and that will peel the hide off you,' said Séamaisín.

'May you not live to see it!' said Séamas.

April 1921

Snow on the Mountains

THERE was a spell of sunshine and it would do your heart good to gaze all around. Mount Brandon had its white cap on, that would suit it on any day in midwinter. What covered it was so white that it made every part of it from the ground up look like chalk. When you grow tired of gazing on that mountain, look south-east and you will see its brother—Macgillycuddy's Reeks. Carrauntoohil is a gleaming white mass, its outlines blurred.

There was not a grain of that heavy snowfall on the fields of the Blasket. The warmth from the ocean is the cause of that, the old people used to say. The sea is warmer than the air when there is frost or snow. Many a time a fisherman pulled off his boots and stockings in the middle of the night on account of the cold and plunged his feet into the sea to warm them.

Séamaisín happened to meet me fairly early.

'Wasn't that a dreadful shower that fell last night,' said he. 'I never experienced the likes before. I fully expected the roof to be riddled with holes from all the lumps of hail that struck it!'

'It won't be melted on those great hills for a week,' said I.

'Oh, there won't be any trace of it left by nightfall with those grand soft spells of sunshine,' said he.

He was proved right.

April 1921

Signs of Foul Weather

TADHG the Joker comes in the door to me. He looks cold and pinched. He brings news about the signs of bad weather brewing and he is shivering, and hunching his shoulders.

'Holy Mary in Heaven!' says he. 'There's no use anyone doing a stroke or struggling to stay alive after the signs of bad weather that are plain to see—a good share of them I never saw before, as far back as I can remember. Otters, instead of living in the great sea, which is their right and proper place, are taking up their stations now in the hills and all over the fields. Don't you see Beiginis white over with sea-gulls—another bad sign; but by the way the world has changed, I suppose it is coming to its end. Seals have been walking the land for a week. Mary, Holy Mother, did anyone ever hear of such a thing, and of many other changes that never appeared before!' says Tadhg.

April 1921

'Leave Work alone unless God is with You'

SINCE the people of this village had been in dire straits for want of good turf for the fire, this year they cut some of it early. Even so, and although good drying weather came along, they had little to show for their efforts because, like all who are in too great a hurry, they stacked it in windrows when it was still too wet. The next time they went out to the turf they found it sprouting again. The first fine day that came, they spread the sods of turf out under the sun once more. The following day the rain came clattering down, but some made the trip to the hill all the same. Before they arrived back home under the drenching flood, they were as wet as the turf themselves.

I met Séamas after he had come from the hill and you may lop the tip of my ear off, but he would not fetch much of a price at Castle Island fair. He had an old, tattered and torn coat on him and I suppose the tailor who made it has been under the ground for many a day. The bush under his nose—that used to keep the flies out of his mouth on a day of sunshine—was catching every drop of water dripping from his cap and letting it stream down onto his chest. His broken boots were spurting white foam with every step he took. You would think washerwomen were below in them.

'You bear the signs of your work on you, Séamas,' said I.

'Oh, leave work alone unless God is with you,' said he.

April 1921

Heat

TODAY is so pleasant that ailing men who have not put their heads outside for a quarter of the year, some for a full year maybe, are now leaning their backs against field-wall or bush, their chests bared to the sun. The lambs are frisking. The dogs' tongues are hanging out a yard. Men and women are stripped to their shirts, their skins white or yellow as God made them.

There is a fever of work in this place such as I have never seen before. They have all the lobster pots in the water now and their tasks piling up on them at once. Furthermore, the women here are fond of tea and mad for tobacco, with the pipe empty maybe, for want of a shilling. There is no credit to be had with life as it is, and now that the lobsters can bring in the shilling to fetch these delights home it is right, surely, for the women to give the men a helping hand to make that extra shilling.

The French fishing boats are causing havoc. They are there off shore at all hours with lobster pots set among our own pots. The women do not like to see them here for they take all and bring them nothing.

April 1921

The Day of the 'Station'[1]

IT is 'Station' day for us. God's messengers have come to visit us. The parish priest left instructions at Dunquin on Sunday that they should be fetched on Monday if it was fine. If not, on the Tuesday. But Monday was glorious on sea and land.

The Islanders were washed and in their Sunday best to meet them. You would think they had never known a poor day. The priests were pleased with them, and they were pleased with each other. The priests were in the Island by seven o'clock in the morning. Two Masses were said and since they had the fine day to spend as they pleased, they were in no great hurry to leave. They bring their own luncheon and all the Islanders have to do is prepare it. The parish priest intends having a month's holiday with us before long.

When they were standing outside on the green near the main road, with the sun shining brightly above their heads, the priests declared that the Island was a wonderful place.

April 1921

---

[1] Mass said in a private house. On the Island it was said in the schoolhouse.

Early Morning Chat

I STROLLED out this morning while it was still quite early. The sun was shining low in the sky. It looked as if it would make a good day for work for the man who was willing and able for it. My habit is to sweep my eyes over the four quarters whenever I put my head outside. In my survey this time I saw at the western end of the White Strand a hearty woman on her way up from the sea. I set off then along the path until we met. She had a bag of sand on her back with an apron-full of strand fare clutched to her breast as she was striding along.

'Isn't it early in the morning you are working, God bless you,' said I to her.

'Holy Mary, this isn't early!' says she. 'I have food cooked already over the turf I fetched down from the hill when it was early.'

*   *   *

The first news I heard early this morning from Raidhrí, an old age pensioner, was of ducks and hens found dead at a neighbour's house after the night.

This was a woman who had not enough hens. One day she said to herself that she was hard done by, not to have enough hens round her hearth, while all her friends on the mainland had plenty. With that thought she jumped into a currach that was going out and spent a week collecting among her relations. Seven hens and a duck she had on her return.

When she arrived home she put the duck in a corner where she had a goose hatching. The hens she put with the five or six other hens she had. Next day her husband went out to inspect his poultry. He searched for the goose. He rushed back in with a startled look in his eyes.

'Your duck has been killed by the goose, my dear woman!' he said.

'The Slaughter of the Dún on you,[1] from which only five came out alive!' she retorted. 'How well it is never good news you tell me any morning.'

April 1921

---

[1] There are two versions of the origin of this Kerry curse. According to the first, 600 Spanish and Papal troops, who had come to assist the Geraldine revolt in 1580 against Elizabethan authority, were massacred at Dún an Óir in nearby Smerwick Harbour by a combined English land and sea force under Lord Grey. The Elizabethan forces included Walter Raleigh and Lord Grey's personal secretary, the poet Edmund Spenser.

The second has it that Piaras Ferriter, the local chieftain/poet, built a false bridge near his 'dún', or castle, on the nearby mainland during the rebellion of 1641, by which means he lured a thousand British soldiers to their destruction.

Trouble in Dingle

NEWS came in that trenches had been dug deep in every road, that the train was not running, that Dingle was without a stone of flour after a hold-up of only one day. Because the Crown Forces were unable to travel through the countryside, they in turn refused to allow any mother's son into the big town. A very awkward state of affairs. Stock and people without a bite to eat. Even if you had permission to go in, there wasn't enough food to spare for a gander. For every man who had enough and to spare, there were five without a crust.

The strike lasted about a week. Motor boats were sent to Tralee for food, which they brought back quickly, but the sentries were guarding Dingle still and no one was allowed in.

When the Islanders heard that the dry roads were blocked, off with them through the road God planned for them the first day ever, and they headed for Dingle across the open sea. The British authorities played their part well. When the leading lights of Dingle explained that it was not the Islanders who had trenched the roads against them, nor was it in their power to do so, they let them take away whatever they wanted and come again and again too!

That set off great squawks of complaint. How did the Islanders manage it? It is an indulgence from God to them, to atone for the hardships that beset them at times when others have a life of ease.

May 1921

Moving a currach up the Blasket slip

The Conger Eel

A FISHERMAN came home and all he had for his day's catch was one conger. When he had stowed away his tackle his wife asked if he had any fish she could cook for the children.

'The devil a one, wisha,' said he, 'except for a single conger out there in the bag. Fetch it in if you are prepared to cook it for them.'

'That I will, faith. I'm glad to have it,' said she.

Off she went out and looked for the bag but she found no conger. Back in she came, bristling at her husband, for she thought he was trying to make a fool of her.

'Look here! There's nothing in that bag, only an old fishing line,' said she.

'But there's a conger in it,' her husband said.

'There is not, nor a sea-trout either.'

Off out with himself, delighted that he was going to prove her wrong, for he had a conger in the bag when he lowered it from his shoulder and why should it not be there still? He up-ended the bag in a trice but it had vanished.

'Mary up in Heaven,' said he to himself, 'what took you out?'

He could find no trace of it, alive or dead.

He had put it into the bag without cutting it or drawing its blood. The upshot was that it had made for the sea again and the next day someone else killed it. The proof was there—the first man's hook was stuck in its jaw.

May 1921

Selling Lobsters in Iveragh

THE boat buying lobsters has stopped calling at the Blasket.
There is no counting the number of lobsters stored away here.
All the Islanders can do is turn the lobster boxes upside down
and dump the lobsters back in the sea and that is a wretched
business after all the trouble the poor men have had.

Éamonn it was who loaded what lobsters he had into his
currach and headed towards Tralee with them, but the wind
changed and he had to veer towards Iveragh. He spent two days
and two nights away from home and there was still no sign of
him returning. I remember a time when there would have been
great lamentation over someone missing as long as he was, but
now the world is so changed that no more tears were shed over
him than over a young rabbit.

When he reached Cahirciveen he found the train was not
running, houses had been burnt down, men were dead, so
lobsters were the last thing on people's minds. Éamonn and his
crew put the lobsters in sacks and went hawking them from door
to door. No one knows what happened, but they came home on
the third day hungry and wretched.

Everyone has given up since. Not a hand or fist is being put in
a lobster pot.

The outlook is not bright, I fear, Gold help us!

Summer 1921

Tadhg Nods Off

TADHG the Joker spent a good stretch of today here with me in my own house and I didn't mind how long it was, for every syllable that passes his lips whiles away the time for you, no matter whether you are burdened with worry or free from care.

Well, we were discussing the affairs of the world when sleep defeated him in the end. It is long since I had to give up reading to him out of any book or newspaper, for no sooner had I the item in my hand than his two eyes were closed and he was in danger of tottering into the fire. Everyone has his own failing.

'Tadhg,' said I to him, 'maybe your dinner is ready and a swallow of good strong tea would do you no harm with the complaint you have—not that it is any bad complaint.'

'The devil sweep it, wisha! It is no good complaint either,' said he.

Up he rose and off out the door with him.

When Tadhg arrived home there was news waiting which did not please him: a grand young ass he had trained had fallen down the cliff at Seal Cove. All the blame was on his own head, for he was the one that said the ass should be let out of the field where he used to spend each night and where he was sure to be found the next morning. As soon as he was given free rein he could not be found.

Everyone said he was worth four pounds and they are scarce at any price.

'The devil take him—and he has done!' said Tadhg. 'If only I had the turf gathered with him at least.'

Summer 1921

A Bull Tethered

A JOBBER came in from Dingle buying stock—sheep, cattle, every class of animal. He saw Raidhrí's bull being driven along the road and he bought him to put out to grass in Beiginis. Raidhrí took him across. He drove a stake into the ground and tethered the bull to it with a rope to prevent him swimming back home, for many is the time animals like him had swum across. Raidhrí left him tethered there for five days and then went to Dingle and collected his money, saying that the bull was as tame as a lamb. When he came home, with the price of the bull in his pocket, he crossed over to Beiginis, pulled up the stake, brought away the rope and let the bull roam free.

No sooner was this done than the bull made off, heading for the sea to swim back to his old haunt. The currach had to turn around and drive him back onto Beiginis again. Seven times they did this, but in the end darkness was falling and they slipped away from the bull.

'There's no knowing whether he'll be there in the morning,' said someone to Raidhrí.

'Let him go to the devil and the west of Ireland! If he has no sense, I have no remedy for him!' was Raidhrí's answer.

But before he had his money safe in his pocket he had a good remedy—a stake and a rope!

Summer 1921

A Cow Takes a Tumble

AFTER hauling five loads of turf home with my old black ass, my labour for the day was done, but the work around the house was still before me: the turf to bring in, water to fetch, a fire to light, a loaf to bake, a diary to write up—so, there were enough chores waiting for an old man in the late evening, or I am greatly mistaken.

I had everything put to rights at last, my pen in my fist, the page started on the blue writing paper, when I jumped into the air. I thought the noise that shook the house was a cannon ball from a warship with the crash that went through my ears. The lamp was lit by this time for it was half-past nine. As I would be on my own in the house I said to myself that it would be strange not to take a look outside before going to bed.

I did so and peered in the exact direction from which I thought the crash had come. What was it but a hulking cow that had fallen into the narrow gap between the back of the house and the hillside, and not a mark or a scratch on her. I was not long gazing down from the bank above the house when two little girls came towards me, one driving a cow, the other with no cow.

'What has happened to your cow?' I asked.

'Oh, she is ahead of me on the path,' said she.

'Look, is that her down there?' said I.

She looked.

'Holy Mary in Heaven, how did she land there?' said she.

Summer 1921

The View from the Pass

It was a fine Sunday. I went for a walk after dinner and since part of my holding is further up at the top end of the village and cattle stray into it now and again, I took my dog along with me. After a tour round the potato plots I strolled up further and not far ahead was the pass called Mám na Leacan. When I stood in the dead centre of this pass I had no way of escaping any sudden squall no matter from which of the four quarters it might be driving.

When I turned to gaze north, there I could see boats fishing away like any other day of the week, but they were not from here, they were from the land of France. There were three of them west at Tiaracht, four north at Inis Tuaisceart, three east at Ferriter's Head and two south at Slea Head.

These are causing great harm and they will cause more, and not in one way only. Besides carrying off the fish, they are weakening the Faith too, for the poor Island fisherman is watching them catching the share of fish that should be his, on a Sunday, which for him is a day of rest.

Summer 1921

Lobster Fishermen far Afield

A CURRACH from the Island loaded up her lobsters and sailed over Dingle Bay to Iveragh. They had a fine evening going out, but the next day, when they thought it was time to return, there was blinding fog, and that is not to be praised at sea.

They sold the lobsters somehow or other, hawking them door to door. I believe a share of them went to some of the old women for the price of a pint of porter.

Well, they were held up the day after that by the heaviest fog that ever came down. They had to dip into the money-chest and draw on it. There was no trouble in up-ending it and they soon had it emptied.

The fog had not lifted the following day either, forcing them to put off their departure again. In the evening of the third day they were being keened over when someone on the hill sighted them about half-way across the bay, after the fog had lifted.

People say that on their third day in Iveragh a collection was taken for them and I can easily credit it. They were changed out of all recognition by the time they reached the landing place. I think it will be a while before these men cross over there again, or anyone else from here either.

Any man who saw the great numbers of lobsters caught in this Island, and no buyer at all coming for them, would pity the fisherman.

July 1921

Home Rule

I WAS coming across the new roadway and a man lives along there who has times when he does not feel well, but when he does feel well, he would make you believe that he could fit wooden legs under chickens for you. I had a stick in my hand at the time, driving my old black ass, with a good day's work in view drawing home the rest of the year's turf. We have been in dire straits over the poor turf for the past three years.

This man was leaning over a wall with his pipe in his mouth, sucking hard on it to draw it, but without result. The pipe ignored his efforts, for no smoke was coming out. It seems he was not able to humour his pipe in the first place by shoving a plug of tobacco in, so the pipe returned the compliment by not giving him a smoke.

Well, I'm telling my story like Tomás Kearney—a long rigmarole with little sense.

'Come over here to me,' said the man with the pipe.

'But I'm in a hurry,' I answered.

'Oh, you can sit by the cinders for yourself now! Haven't we won Home Rule.'

'How did we come by it, or what sort of rule is it?'

'Oh, *republic*,' said he.

'I don't understand. Say the word in Gaelic.'

'I can't.'

'And it was little sleep you lost over winning it either!' was the answer I made.[1]

July 1921

[1] A truce in the Anglo–Irish War came into operation on 11 July 1921 and negotiations for an Anglo–Irish Treaty began in London.

The Four Sheep

MANY of us had congregated together, as we used to hear Mass every morning around nine o'clock and the men would stand around waiting for the priest to come.[1]

'Did you get a good price for the sheep yesterday, Éamonn?' one man asked another who had just come back from Dingle where he had taken sheep to market.

'It would be no use my telling you, for you wouldn't believe me.'

'Maybe I'm not in the habit of believing you or any other windbag like you.'

'Well, I'll tell the other men here and maybe someone might believe me,' said Éamonn.

He started telling his rigmarole.

'I had four sheep in Dingle yesterday, and those four were the equal of any four sheep I've ever sold for the past four years, and during all that time I never sold any four, but those four the last day were every bit as good. Every four sheep during that time fetched twelve pounds for me, but the last lot only brought five pounds. How much am I out of pocket?'

'Seven pounds,' a pert youngster standing there chimed in.

'A kick of God's curse on their backsides!' said Tadhg, referring to the sheep buyers.

July 1921

---

[1] Visiting priests on holiday in the summer said Mass every day in the schoolhouse.

Ignorant Comment

DÓNALL meets me.

'Are yeer potatoes any good?' I ask.

'They are famous, except they are no size, but I never saw "Blacks" on this Island better for eating.'

'You're strolling around for yourself like any gentleman,' says I.

'That isn't much to my credit, for it is no way to be for a man who has his wits about him.'

'But 'tis no reflection on a man to have his work in hand, and until you had it safely behind you, you did not spend your time strolling around,' says I.

'They all have their work in hand, but it isn't strolling around they are because they have their wits about them and are busy fishing for themselves.'

Dónall's news was that the Irish negotiations in London were breaking down.

We had not been long conversing together in this way when an old age pensioner went by along the path. 'Coachman' is the nickname they have for him. He has a beard like a goat's whiskers and every bristle is as tough as the tooth of a hackle. He cocked his head on one side, saying 'By all accounts ye are doing well in London.' Now, I dislike listening to ignorant comment like that, the more so from an old man, so I asked:

'Where did you hear the oracle?'

'The men told me.'

'There isn't one of them but is completely in the dark still about what is going on over there,' was the answer I made.

July 1921

On Mullach Reamhar

It was a grand day altogether for autumn. I fixed the panniers on my old black ass, for I have a quantity of turf in the place they call Mullach Reamhar. This lies westwards about half-way down the length of the Island and it is very rugged ground to travel, but the best top sod of turf in Ireland is there, to my thinking.

Well, when I reached Mullach I thought it no waste of time to spend a while gazing around and by the time I left off gazing, I felt the value of a cow had been added onto my health, it had so much improved. A fishing boat from France was crossing the Great Sound in a southerly direction, on its way home full of lobsters and crayfish. Another boat from England rode at anchor off Inishvickillaun, waiting to pay ten shillings a dozen for crayfish and lobsters from the currachs which could be seen in every inlet and ravine there.

A misty white haze rose from the sea at this time, floating over the round-topped hills. The plants on the hillside were not without their own sweet scent. You need not stir from where you stood on the height to fill your lungs with the scented breeze, from whichever quarter it might be blowing. I used to wonder why city folk would make for a place like this, but I need not have wondered.

September 1921

'There is no Limit to What Money can do'

THIS is the first day earning money at the work made available for the poor. The first place they tackled was Gravel Strand to make a good trackway down to the gravel for the women and asses to use. Thirty-three pounds a week is allocated to the Island. I don't know how long it will last. A man from every house is employed. The pay is a crown a day. If you saw them all heading for the strand along the top and bottom roads, every man shouldering his own implement, you would swear there were not so many men living on the Island.

They have begun a fine trackway there now, and hard work it is too, since the only implements they have are the shovel and spade, both digging as hard as they can. The overseer is an Islandman. The other creeks will be dealt with afterwards —some occupation will always be found so long as the money lasts.

''Tis ever said,' said Séamas, 'that there is no limit to what money can do. That's a fine piece of work altogether done for seven pounds.'

'I suppose, Séamas, it would be a long while before you grew tired of earning a crown a day.'

'Never in all my life,' said he. 'My grandfather was a good man and he worked for sixpence a day.'

September 1921

Men carrying a currach

Bloom and Blossom

I TURNED for home with five or six fish, my first day out fishing this year. I was thankful I was no 'glab', as they always call a fisherman without a catch. Síle was digging potatoes and I asked her if she was pleased with them.

'I pulled up a stalk with forty potatoes under it and every one of them would go through the eye of a needle,' said she. 'Virgin Mary, isn't it a great wonder that there is no crop and the blue blossoms still on them!'

'But seeing how your own bloom has faded from you, aren't you glad that the blossom is on your potatoes, Síle?'

'Holy Mary, my bloom is vanished. Look at my hair today as white as chalk, and not even half of it left, compared to the lovely golden locks I had on me once of a day.

'By my baptism,' said she again, 'whatever number of grey hairs I have, they will grow greyer still unless it is God's will to send me a handful of good potatoes, for there is no other pound or sixpence to be earned.'

Up she springs out of the trench, plunges her hand into her pocket, pulls out a match, plunges her hand in again and hauls out a clay pipe as black as coal.

She reddened it.

'We must make the most of what we have,' said she.

On my reckoning she must have spent fifteen pounds on tobacco for her pipe by this stage of her life.

September 1921

A Clean Sweep of Séamas's Potatoes

'Iᴛ is seldom you would see a cat with a saddle on him'—and it is just as seldom you would catch me rising early for the past few years. This morning, however, I was up good and early, for I had a notion that seaweed was there to be gathered. I had my drop of tea swallowed, my pipe puffing well, stuffed full with the sweet-scented tobacco from the gentleman who sent it—may God reward him.[1]

I set off on my journey then heading west towards the strands. As I walked on I was gazing at the potato plots on this side and that. The day was not light enough yet to see clearly, but when I reached Séamas's field I was amazed to see all the asses gathered in the one field. It startled me to find them there, the more so since I knew that the potatoes Séamas had been digging for the past week had not been gathered up yet. I set the dog on them and he roused them, driving them all down onto the strand. I followed, for I had not laid an eye on my own old ass for three days. He was with them, of course. Every ass on the Blasket was there except three. That meant twenty-six. They were the great harvesters to be in the one field all night long. There was not a solitary potato left after them this morning.

September 1921

---

[1] Brian O'Kelly.

A Ship's Prow Submerged

I⊤ looks like the depths of winter. Showers of heavy rain and
wind from the north-west, and by the way it is driving I think
there will be few blossoms left on Síle's potatoes, whatever
bloom is on herself.

When I put my head out at the height of the morning, I saw
two steamships ploughing northwards through the tide. They
kept pace with each other at full speed without slackening.
There was a strong raging spring tide running. A flood tide was
swirling northwards past Beiginis Head. The ship behind was
aware of nothing until the water was washing over the one in
front back to its mizzen-mast. Before she could slacken speed
herself, she too was awash up to the helm. They slackened speed
then like two fools, making headway in no direction. For half an
hour they made no move at all, north or south. Finally they
turned south running before the gale and fetched the grand
broad bay of Ventry.

'It is small wonder that a little currach would have to turn
back out of the storm,' said an old man who put his head outside
the door and saw them turning. 'But these have the foresight
Dónall Óg was lacking that time in Dingle, when he spent three
pounds ten on the drink and next day hadn't a shred of tobacco
to put in his pipe. Steer clear of any man who doesn't keep his
wits about him in Dingle,' said he.

September 1921

Repairing the Well

THERE is news on the mainland that the parish priest had money for people who are badly off; it was not available as charity, but to be earned with a little work. Sixty pounds was coming to the priest each week, earmarked for Dunquin and the Island. Half was sent to the Island and work was started both there and on the mainland. There was nearly war among them in both places over who would be given work and who left idle. The pay was a crown a day and the overseer was local, so you can be sure there was no great sweat. The work went on for four days in the week, with the other two working days idle.

Every man had earned two pounds by the time the work came to an end and another pound was owed to them. The money ceased when the fishing started.

The Yank's Well was the first place repaired with the money. Twenty pounds was spent on it, I believe. It was built up with stones and a man would take three hours to carry one stone to the well—a stone that you could have flung over the house with one hand! It is repaired now, but Diarmaid's wife spent a week without swallowing a drop of tea, for fear the water was not clean enough after being disturbed.

They are still not satisfied with it, for the geese flock round there.

September 1921

The Dog's Plight

WELL, whether it be sense or folly to confess it, I may as well admit that no one else in the world was to blame but myself, and the dog was mine.

When I got him first as a pup he was a good-sized animal, but he wasn't much to look at. As I had no other dog on the hearth I said to myself: 'Bad as Séamas is, we would be worse off without him.' The gaunt look of him softened me too, I dare say, however ungainly he was.

It wasn't long before he turned into a fine dog, since he had the run of the house like a pet, and soon afterwards I noticed how mournful he looked whenever I didn't call him to accompany me out. It seemed odd to me then to leave him a prey to this disease when the remedy was in my own hands, so I let him follow at my heels every day from then on.

Swimming was the first lesson I taught him and, if the student were as proficient in learning his Gaelic lesson as the dog was in swimming, Ireland would not be without her language.

On this particular day I picked up my fishing line and took crab for bait. I was following my usual practice, for it is a long time now since I did any proper fishing. When I had the line ready I cast it in the hope of making a catch, but no sooner had it struck the water than my dog shot after it. He caught the bait in his mouth, hook and all, and he ran towards me to drop it at my feet.

This was more hindrance than help to me, for I had to take the knife to the side of his mouth to cut away the hook.

Now, when all was ready once more, I cast the line again and warned the dog not to go near it. He made no stir. I had a float attached to the line and, whatever way I was fumbling about, what did I see when I raised my head but my float drifting away and no sign of my line! I called to the dog to go out after the float and fetch it to me, which he did on the instant.

It was then I saw that something had been caught. A huge conger eel of a man's length it was. I had it hauled well up the shore when it snapped off the hook and started down to the sea again. Off with the dog after it. It grabbed the dog's snout, dragged him out and dived down to the bottom with him. My dog never came back up again.

Very reluctantly I went up home without fish or dog—my good companion. May the curse of the twenty-four men fall on the catfish that snatched him from me! If I had three pound notes in my pocket I would pay them to have him back. I never went in that direction since, although it is many the string of rock-fish the gentlemen[1] used to see me bringing up out of there, after I had spent a while in their company each day.

October 1921

---

[1] Visitors learning Gaelic.

Two Ships

A LARGE, beautiful, gleaming, well-equipped vessel was sailing north-east of Ceann Sratha and Cúl le Beann. The people here never saw her equal before for size and splendour. As she majestically held her northerly course from Barra Liath, a great warship came from the south through the Blasket Sound. She was steaming ahead and caught up with the other vessel off Fiach an Fhirtéaraigh. The two sailed out of our sight. The merchant ship was from America, you can be sure, and she carried a mighty cargo, whatever it was. Tralee or Limerick was her destination by the course she was steering.

The fishing has failed in this place for a fortnight past and the poor men will be without a sixpence or a pound. They have no way of living and all they can do is place themselves in God's hands and He is good, praise be to Him for ever. It is often He bestowed plenty on people when they were least expecting it.

'How do ye know but that a ship might run upon the rocks and provide ye with plenty, like the "Quebra",[1] said Séamas, 'so that we managed for three years as a result.'

'But vessels like that don't always run upon the rocks when there is need of them,' said Séamaisín.

'Whist, uncle,' said Séamas, 'maybe there might be one on the White Strand by morning!'

October 1921

---

[1] Ship that foundered off the Island during the Great War.

Heavy Fishing and Light Money

THE sea was alight everywhere with fish shoaling. The weather was very fine and everyone was equipped and ready for the night. Most of the currachs made their catch when day brightened and every currach and boat afloat netted it around the Blasket coast only. Nowhere else were the shoals so dense, I believe. Some of the currachs took their catch to Dingle Harbour, some to Ventry Harbour and others to Dunquin. Most of them had netted three thousand mackerel. The Dunquin men had to haul it up to the horse-drawn carts on the cliff top—hard work after the night.

Four and sixpence the hundred was what the fishermen made in Dunquin. It was six shillings in Dingle. The carters charged one and sixpence a hundred to transport it from Dunquin.

The following night there was not a fish to be caught and only the merest handful ever since.

Séamas happened to meet me.

'It will not make a good year, my sweet man,' said he.

'How so, Séamas?'

'Oh, I have every reason for saying so,' said he. 'There is no potato in the ground that is not shrivelled up. There is no fish to be caught and even if a man could catch any, it would take a while for him to make five pounds at the price it is fetching now.'

'That is a point, Séamas, but the price of flour is coming down.'

'No matter,' said he, 'even if it fell to a crown, seeing that the same crown is out of our reach.'

October 1921

Every Currach Full

EVERY currach all along the coast was full to the brim with mackerel. In Árd na Caithne harbour the seine-nets were weighted down to the sea bottom with fish. There never was such a show or spectacle as the amount of fish on its way to Dingle. A large quantity of it was bought at a shilling a hundred. That shilling did not pay the cost of the cartage; it was sixpence short. But the man who caught the fish did not receive the shilling, nor even so much as a penny. Not a single sixpence reached the Island out of that day's fishing, although every currach there was loaded to the gunwhale.

The carters refused to transport it to town from the harbour for there was a glut and it would not pay them. The Islanders could not buy salt either, for the shopkeepers who had been selling it at a crown the hundredweight charged fifteen shillings for it when they saw the plight the people were in.

So there was nothing for it but to pluck the fish out of the nets and pitch them back dead into the sea. Many said that, if the gates of Paradise lay open for the crowd selling the salt to pass through, you could be sure that all who ever died had gone in before them.

We have our own rogues in this country seven times worse than those in lands abroad and, if Ireland were entirely independent from every country in the world, she would never amount to anything on account of the pack of scoundrels here.

October 1921

Winter Storm

IT is a winter's day and shows all the marks of it. The blast of the great gale is driving the waves high over all that lies within their reach. The rocks jutting out of the sea are smothered by the fury of the white surf bursting over them. The grass that yesterday was green is withered today. The very skin on the people is changing with the bad weather. The sheep on the hillside are blown from their pastures and are trying to push their way in the door to us. The fish that all summer disported itself and basked in the sun near the surface of the water has vanished in the storm. The young woman, trim as a swan on the lake for the rest of the year, brings in her bucket of water; with the comb snatched from the back of her head by the wind, her hair trailing into her mouth, her clothes spattered with mud, the water half spilt, she is as ill-humoured as someone who is out of tobacco.

Of the old people, whose bones were so smooth and supple all summer in the warmth of the sun, this one has cramp in his leg, that one's arm is paining him and another is dozing by the fire with an eye being kept on him for fear he might fall in.

There is great healing in fine weather, and great harm follows the bad.

November 1921

Returning from the Dance

A DANCE was held over in Dunquin and there was a great gathering. Two currachs had also gone out full from the Blasket. Maitiú from the Island was the fiddler they had. There was singing and dancing until nine o'clock the next morning. Each lad paid three shillings for the entertainment and each girl paid two. The fiddler received a guinea. 'A gay night and a sorry milking time' they had, as the saying goes.

Next day, Sunday, there was rain and high wind. Anyone roaming beyond the bounds of his own parish got more than he bargained for. The rain water lashed down and the sea water lashed up on the Islanders returning home. There were eight girls in the two currachs, with the waves breaking over them. Every stitch covering their bones was as drenched as if they had fallen into the sea. Many people were waiting for them above the landing place, each with his own comment:

' 'Tis my opinion, my sweet man,' said Séamas, 'that there are some people who are short of sense; and I think the same applies to those who did not stay at home for themselves.'

'I suppose,' retorted Séamaisín, 'they must strike you as odd, since you never ventured into such a place yourself. You had too much sense for that, to your way of thinking. But what have you gained by all your sense today? You are an old wasted 'lone bird', without wife or child. Isn't it often a person brought a good life's partner away from such a house, a partner he or she would never have met, if they followed your example and stayed at home.'

They all burst out laughing.

November 1921

Horns on the Pooka

I WAS digging a few potatoes when a student strolled up to me. The story he had was that the Pooka had been seen the night before by three lads, and said he:

'He had a pair of horns on him, but does the Pooka have horns, I wonder?'

'I never heard he has,' said I, 'but anything outside the creatures of this world with horns on him can only come from the place down below.'

Later in the day I enquired into it more closely and heard the full story. A couple of lads had been out setting snares to catch rabbits. As the moon had risen and was shedding its light, three others made for the hill to steal the rabbits out of the snares set by the first two. The pair noticed them slipping off, so they took a short cut themselves and were lying in wait for the three in the spot where the snares had been set. They had a white sheet and two poles. One of them wrapped the sheet round himself and pushed the two poles out through it. He was not long dressed in this disguise when the thieves arrived. They thought at first it was a sheep with a big white fleece and horns, until the figure spoke in a loud voice:

'The man in the middle is the man I want!'

That was the apparition of the Pooka. That was the moment of terror. The three were scarcely able to make it back home and they were far from looking themselves.

November 1921

Blasket harbour. Seán 'Sheaisí' Kearney can be distinguished on the left

Tadhg has a New Ass

IT is Sunday, a cold hard day with a wind blowing. Some of the currachs went out to Mass all the same. A man from the Island had gone out to the mainland three days earlier looking for an ass to buy. The man is Tadhg the Joker and he is often in search of asses. I don't mean that as a reproach. He is better off on a quest for them than on a quest for his health. This time he found one without any trouble, though often before he had spent a week away from home on the search and, often too, that was a week spent in vain.

It was in the parish of Ventry that he came across this ass and paid thirty shillings for him. Whatever explanation there is for it, he never found one yet but he would be up to pranks, like Tadhg himself.

Now, at the time when the currachs were making to head home Tadhg drove the ass down to the landing place in Dunquin and let him roam loose along the shore where everything was heaped ready to stow in the boats. After a while, one of the men happened to glance up and what did he see but the ass ripping and tearing a half-sack of flour belonging to some poor man and the flour scattered all over the shore.

When Tadhg saw the mischief caused by the ass: 'Oh, wisha, the curse of the twenty-four men fall on you!' said he, and he made for him and would have killed him, but for one of his sons who was nearby.

November 1921

The New Ass Astray

TADHG fixed the panniers on the new ass and, at a steady pace, drew a load of turf from Mullach Reamhar, which is a good step from home. It was dinner time when they reached the house. While Tadhg was eating his own food he gave food to the ass too. Afterwards he wanted the ass to become accustomed to the 'estate'. With his pipe stuck in his mouth and a staff in his hand, Tadhg drove him ahead, having high notions of showing the land to his new steed. When he came to the roadside he saw his mistake: he had brought no rope to tie the ass in the field. Tadhg hurried back home for it, but by the time he returned to the roadside where he had left the ass, there was no trace of him. He stuck his finger in his mouth and blew a whistle that carried all over the village. Everyone poked his head out under the impression that it was a ship passing through the Blasket Sound, for it is often they blow their whistle in greeting to us. Often too Tadhg had played the same trick on them.

He gave a roar out of him to know if anyone had news of the ass, but they had not. He shouted to his wife, telling her to go east and he would search to the west himself. But neither of them came upon the ass. He had just whipped his hat off to start cursing the animal when he saw him down on the White Strand.

'Drown and be damned to you!' says Tadhg.

November 1921

Blind Creek Point

IT was Sunday and for a winter's day it would not be easy to find a day to surpass it, it was so fine. There was no cloud in the sky and you could not conceive there would be ever again.

Around midday I picked up a small prayer book and turned my back on the house to go and read the book in a spot where the sun was shining at the far end of the cultivated plots.

I did not stop in my stride until I reached Boat Creek Point. There is no corner of the capital city of Ireland that I would prefer to that grassy spot where I now sat down.

When I wearied of the book I strolled as far as Blind Creek Point. There I had the sight to see. I suppose, may God forgive me, if I had gone to that point first, I would be without rosary or prayer out of my little book that day.

The first sight that met my eyes was dancers: three groups, a set distance apart from each other, performing an eight-hand reel. Another surprise for me: there was no lad amongst them. Facing each group of dancers, a young lass sat on a low wall lilting for them. A man of discernment would travel far to listen to them, their voices were so sweet. When I quickened my step towards the cliff overlooking Gravel Strand, it was down there the lads were, in their shirt sleeves, kicking football.

November 1921

A Currach in the Midst of the Storm

THIS is the day that Éamonn was to come back from the Lesser Blaskets where he had spent three days rabbiting. It was a wild day with showers and a strong wind except that the wind was behind him and he ran before it. All the same a heavy sea was running and the currach could not carry her sail. A crowd of people had gathered on the hill to watch the cockle-shell boat struggling through the smother. The sea would pour right into her and the breaking wave would sweep one of his dogs over the side. There were ten dogs aboard and the sea swept them all away except one. The currach was carrying fifteen dozen rabbits and that was a heavy load. Few expected him to come safe through it. But he did. It is a long time since any boat from the Island ran through such great peril. Éamonn said that but for the load on board she would have capsized. The weight had kept a hold on the water. When the rabbits were thrown out onto the slip you would swear that they were drowned rats, and the crew were as drenched as they were.

Another currach came in from Dunquin through the same tempest, except that the sea was not quite so rough, for the Great Island breaks the force of the wind in the Sound between itself and Dunquin.

The crew brought news that the terms of the Truce had been broken.

December 1921

A Special Night

THERE is a bright moon in the sky and the night as clear as day. If you stuck your head out around ten o'clock you would imagine you were in the capital city of Ireland with the noise and din of the children playing at 'hide-and-seek', 'the fox', and all the old Irish games they can think of. There is no bed-time for them on such a night until it strikes twelve.

Tonight is a special night for them and they are rushing around in rare elation since a newspaper came in carrying the announcement that the two countries had signed a Treaty[1]. The youngsters caught the excitement from the talk of their elders and they have run wild all over the village. And, I promise you, the news gave a lift to the heart in young and old alike. I dare say there are few among them who object to the settlement and it is hard to fault it.

Just when I had picked up the pen to write this, two little girls ran in the door, their cheeks glistening. I asked them why the sweat was pouring out of them or what was all the pother about. The answer they made was that they were playing games all over the roadways. Séamaisín was taken unawares when he came across some of them a little way from the houses. His first thought was that they were not of this world. When he discovered they were he commented:

'If they keep on like this some of them will have to be tethered.'

December 1921

---

[1] Anglo-Irish Treaty, 6 December 1921.

Séamaisín's Plight with the Seal

ON my way west Séamaisín came towards me with a huge seal on his back.

'Where did you come across the seal, Séamaisín? Is it dead you found him?'

'No, but he nearly left me dead,' said Séamaisín. 'I was entering the cave at Boat Creek to look for seaweed and what did I find above there but my boyo fast asleep. I stepped back and pondered how to come at him. The plan I made was to find two stalks of seaweed with thick ends. Off back in with me, only to find that he was waking up and starting to head straight for the water. I made a drive for him to fetch him a couple of blows that would knock him out, but instead of that he had never been so wide awake as he was after the seven blows I dealt him. Beating him with the stalks of seaweed was like beating him with a goose-quill.

'In the end he grabbed my stalks of seaweed and chewed them up. I turned around then looking for a stone, but while I had my back to him he had crept up on me and had taken a grip on the calf of my leg. He took a mouthful out of it. I have the seal for I struck him with the stone, but the seal will have me, for my leg will never mend till Judgment Day.'

December 1921

Memory and Melancholy

AROUND midday where did I find myself standing but on exactly that green grassy point between Boat Creek and Blind Creek. There my dawdling came to a halt and, although I have been there often since my first visit long ago, at this hour it was as perfect as I had seen it on any previous occasion when I had planted my two feet there. Then I started pacing up and down, to and fro, on the point. The sun was shining bright without a puff of wind in the sky; the murmur of the sea rose and fell pleasantly; no wildness now, no raging. The birds on sea and land were chattering together with every sign that they understood each other, for some would fly out and others fly in. On every hummock and grassy perch where I used to sit with the gentleman[1] who was with me four years ago I placed my hand three times, and if I did not feel more sadness from it than gladness, I did not feel less.

A feeling of loneliness comes over a man on a fine balmy day like this, when there is no one else around to disturb him, and he feels affection for the man who was his comrade and who is far away from him now. Then he grows melancholy. I sat down on a low wall where we used to have that book *Séadna*[2] open and, on my oath, it did not increase my joy—it was driving me further to the other extreme.

Roused from my thoughts by catching sight of Séamaisín with a bundle of seaweed on his back, I walked home with him.

December 1921

---

[1] Brian O'Kelly.
[2] A Gaelic folk-novel by Fr. Peter O'Leary, author of *My Story* (Oxford, 1987).

The Four Pensioners

I Took a stroll west along the path. I made for the cliff above the strand and saw four men below, out in the sea up to their necks gathering seaweed as fast as they could, vying with each other. I peered hard to make out who they were and they proved to be four of our old age pensioners.

Who should come along while I was sitting there but Tadhg the Joker. He gazed down, had a good look at them and recognized them.

'May ye not live another day beyond this!' exclaimed Tadhg. 'And may the crowd that are paying ye the pension go blind, when there are poverty-stricken people elsewhere without a penny in the world.'

'I dare say, Tadhg, you would not easily find four old age pensioners in Ireland stronger, fitter and healthier than they are,' said I.

'Yerra, man, you would not, nor wherever the Crown of the Saxons rules. These are fellows that never used to do a stroke of work until the pension money scattered their senses for them!'

'Isn't it a grand winter's day and a great wonder that not many Islanders are going out to fetch the fare for Christmas,' said he.

'"Foul wind follows fair", Tadhg.'

'How so?'

'Money is not plentiful with poor people and don't you know that the Dingle shopkeepers are mad for money.'

'Oh, wisha, to the devil with half of them! They are notorious!'

Before Christmas 1921

'I don't know whether Ireland's Future is Settled yet?'

'Two days, that's all it is to Christmas,' said Séamas, who joined me on the cliff above the strand, 'and it is on top of the people here before they are ready for it.'

'That is something that never happened in this Island before, Séamas, and it would not happen now either, if they had been able to go to Dingle to buy in provisions, but they were not.'

'Oh, there's something in what you say, for they expected to have a night catching mackerel before Christmas to earn the pennies, but they have neither one thing nor the other.'

'Did anybody ever put this to you, Séamas?'

'What's that?'

'No law ever surpassed God's law. God has the mackerel in His keeping and Christmas Night is marked out to give Him honour. Some people in this world presume to lay down their own rules but that is not in their power. If they wished to pay due honour to Christmas Night they wouldn't be brooding over mackerel flicking their tails in the high sea. Who knows, God might send the fish to them after Christmas.'

'I don't know whether Ireland's future is settled yet?' said he.

'It makes no difference to you whether or which. You would be in the same case if there was a King over every one of the provinces. You are a drenched and pitiable creature in this place every day, reduced to only one meal a day at times.'

'Wisha, by my baptism, my darling man, that's my case, near enough. The pensioners now—look at them: there's no holding them since they got that same pension!' said he.

Before Christmas 1921

Tomás O'Crohan

The Wren's Day[1]

JUST now, when I was writing away, with my small lamp on the
table, who should come in the door to me but half a dozen lads.
Each had a stout stick in his hand; they had masks over their
faces and were dressed up, with their voices disguised, as they
romped up and down the floor. They had what looked like a
little bird on top of a stick and one of them pointed his finger at
it, showing me that they were 'out with the Wren'. Twopence I
gave them. They all went down on their knees thanking me. If
they had the look of devils when they came in, the twopence
changed it to a look of angels.

The day after Christmas 1921

---

[1] St. Stephen, tried by the Sanhedrin for blasphemy, was stoned to death. It
was believed that his hiding place had been betrayed by the chattering of wrens.
Boys in Ireland used to kill wrens and display them when they went round as
mummers on St. Stephen's Day (Boxing Day).

A Man Drowned on the Ridge of the Hill

WHEN I put my head out I heard Tadhg the Joker ranting away in the yard. I went to see what the cause of all the commotion was. He had just come from the hill with his ass and a load of turf. Anyone who saw him at that moment would swear that he and the ass had both come through the raging sea.

Nell stuck her head out.

'Virgin Mary, what happened to you?' said she. 'Sure it isn't a drop of rain or grain of snow we had since morning, but both yourself and the ass are drowned.'

'By Our Lady, my dear woman,' says Tadhg, 'the raging sea drowned us on the ridge of the hill and I dare say the likes never happened before. The place where we have the rick of turf is twelve hundred feet above sea-level and the sea swept over myself and the ass up there.'

'Yerra, no one would believe that blather from you,' said his wife, ''tis how yourself and the ass must have fallen in some hole.'

'Not at all, the devil to it,' said he, 'but the sea is sweeping over the hills and it was touch and go whether I would live to see another Big Supper Night[1] in this world ever again, or the ass either.'

The moment he had finished speaking, a ship's siren was heard being sounded long and soft and sweet.

'That's a vessel,' said someone.

'You must know it is not,' said Nell, 'when a man and an ass were drowned by the raging sea on the ridge of the hill.'

Tadhg put his head out.

'The devil himself couldn't drown them!' he said, when he saw the vessel.

After Christmas 1921

---

[1] New Year's Eve.

New Year's Eve

THE last day of the year and if Tadhg had not gone to fetch turf yesterday, he would not be 'drowned' today. The asses of the village have never stopped drawing loads of turf from the hill since day brightened, for it is a grand dry day; but the sea is not calm yet. A ship has passed through the Sound and that is a very welcome sign for the Islanders to behold. These sea-farers, they say, can read the weather better than anyone.

It was around eight o'clock in the night that I was writing this. I stuck my head out and gazed all around at the parish of Dunquin. After reflecting for a while, many a thought had run through my mind. There were candles lit in the windows wherever your eye would fall, in places that for the rest of the year were black and dark, except on these holy nights. See how the reverence has endured down the generations and will, undoubtedly, for evermore.

New Year's Eve 1921

New Year's Day

THE first day of the New Year and a fine day too. Eight currachs crossed over to the mainland for Mass. The funeral of a man who had relations on the Island was taking place too, so they made a day of it. Some of the young men in Dunquin gave an invitation to Maitiú to go out on Saturday and play his fiddle for them, because they were to have a gathering that night.

In the course of Saturday Maitiú made no move to set off for he was expecting from hour to hour that the young men on the Island would be heading out, but they made no stir. Late in the day the Islanders sighted a currach approaching rowed by four men. No one knew why they were coming, so all in the village were on the cliff waiting for them. Who was it they came to fetch but Maitiú. He did not refuse, but got himself ready and went off with them.

It was after their departure that everyone had his own say.

'By my baptism!' said Tadhg, 'a man without a skill is lost. See how they picked out the fellow with the skill from all the rest.'

'Didn't you know that before now?' said Séamaisín who was standing there. 'And maybe he might be rewarded in more ways than one for his journey. Isn't he a sturdy bachelor, hale and hearty still, and how do you know but a fine strapping woman would walk out the door with him.'

They laughed loud and long.

'It is a marvel how long it's taking one of them to step out by his side,' said another.

'There is time enough yet,' declared Séamaisín.

New Year's Day 1922

Poor Women's Rock

SIX young girls called in to me, and the bumper Christmas edition of *Misneach*[1] was on the window-sill. One of them picked it up. There were a couple of verses of a song in it and she sang them exquisitely from the page and to exactly the right air. It would be hard to find a small girl so young who would be more gifted for singing the verses. That is no wonder, for it is the sound of Gaelic that filled her ears as soon as she appeared in this world and, from then on, it was the roar of the sea and the moaning of the north wind that entered her head through both ears day and night. Each of the girls took her turn at the song, but in any gathering there is one who excels.

'Did ye hear any news since morning?'

'We did, boy! Maybe you didn't hear it yet.'

'What is it, little girl?'

'It's about six girls that went onto Poor Women's Rock and they never noticed the time passing, while they were gathering limpets on the Rock, until the water had filled up the creek.'

'But who noticed they were there, or who rescued them?'

'They came off by themselves, by my palms,' said she, 'when the tide had gone out again.'

'They were a good while there, I suppose.'

'From breakfast in the morning until dinner time, for no one passed that way until then and it was my grandfather, driving the cow west, that saw them. But they were after coming in from the Rock by then and their clothes were drowned wet.'

'I suppose they had an appetite for their dinner, darling,' said I.

'I suppose they did, and an almighty hunger,' said she.

Beginning of January 1922

[1] *Gaelic League Journal.*

A currach

War Over There is not the Same as Here

THIS is the day that Maitiú came home following the dance in Dunquin, after spending four days over on the mainland where he was held stormbound, along with another fellow. The pair of them were returning together at twilight.

The whole village was waiting for them to ask them all the news, especially about the question of peace. There was a majority of five in favour of accepting the Treaty, if the report was true.[1] That partly satisfied the Islanders. Maybe they would have some trade if life were settled. One man said that life was good on the Island before, when the Great War was being waged in France. Maybe there would be another war too and God would load a fine valuable vessel over in the United States and would steer her onto Lóchar Rock as He had steered the 'Quebra'.

'May you be struck blind!' said Séamaisín. 'Surely a war going on in France is not the same as one in your own country, you stump of a fool!—and there is no other word for you, if you suppose that a war in Ireland would make you grow fat. Maybe if the fight was on, you would be no great prop in her defence.'

'I wouldn't go fighting at all if I could stay out of it,' said the other man.

'If you go, may you never come back!' said Séamaisín.

Beginning of January 1922

---

[1] Vote in Irish Parliament on Anglo-Irish Treaty on 7 January. Actually the majority in favour was seven.

Fear of the Future

SEVERAL of the men are on the green. After sending the cattle up the hill they stand chatting together. They are completely idle without any occupation but to go to Diarmaid's house and be arguing with each other until someone would mention it was time for dinner. Then they would bestir themselves to go home and in the evening return again until ten o'clock.

They are very fearful that this will be a poor year for them. They thought they would have some occupation when they heard that peace had been made, but since they hear now that it is breaking down they are losing hope. From Christmas on they would normally be busy making ready the gear for lobsters, but they are reluctant to make a start. Gathering the gear is a big expense if there was no call for the catch; but they have no confidence for it since they heard that the countries would not be at peace. I never knew them so fearful about how to make a living until now. They were not half so worried when the fighting started, but now when the call for peace has come, they take it to heart that it is not instantly made.

When they are arguing together the noise in the house equals that in the great Dáil—one man asserting that there is still time to secure peace, another saying there is not and never will be.

January 1922

Bad News from the Mainland

TODAY the currach that went to Dingle with sheep came back again. All the Islanders were waiting for it. It was its third day away from home. The crew were questioned about the Free State, but it was a confused enough answer they gave. People in favour of the Free State hadn't a word to say, but those against it were beside themselves with rage. The same story all over Ireland, I suppose. People thought there would be no more strife but it looks very much as if there will be now.[1]

It is down on the strands the people of this Island are at this time gathering seaweed. I make my own journey west there. I spread clumps of it on the Field of the White Strand. It is not out of greed for the potatoes that I do it, but I'm looking after my health. I would be in better health there, working constantly, than in any other field of mine doing no work at all.

January 1922

[1] Country drifting into the Civil War (1922–1933) between opponents and supporters of the Anglo–Irish Treaty.

'That is Something I do not Believe!'

Two men who had been on the mainland for three days came in from Dunquin. They had travelled as far afield as Annascaul, in search of withes to make lobster pots, because all those in the neighbourhood had been snapped up. They were not expected back for the waves were bursting up over the green grass everywhere. However, they landed in the course of the evening. There was a heavy swell out at sea and inshore it was worse. They could not have landed were it not for all those waiting for them at the slip, who lifted them out, currach and men together.

The expense had been heavy on them before they reached home. Often in recent years there has been more outlay than profit in lobsters. Every hundred withes they brought back cost half a crown. The expense of the journey on top of this; another day spent bringing them home; a week making the pots; ropes, floats and tar—more expense. It is a big outlay equipping each currach by the time they are ready for duty.

They had heard that England's forces were leaving Ireland's shores because all was peaceful now.

'That is something I do not believe!' said a man standing there, 'for I'm deafened from hearing that they have gone and look how not one of them has left the country yet.'

'I suppose Ireland will be at peace twice over by the time they make any move to go,' said Séamas. 'There will be no true peace in this country until you hear that those fellows have been back home in England for a month.'

January 1922

Echo of Sorrow

IT is blowing hard and cold from the north with the occasional scatter of hail. A currach had been out on the mainland since yesterday but it was not expected back as the day was wild. Late in the evening, with only the mast left standing, it just managed to reach home. The crew had been in Dingle but they had no news of peace in Ireland.

One man argued that the two sides on the Treaty would come to blows now, once the man over the sea had withdrawn. Many agreed with him, only an odd one dissenting. Another said that it was not so easy to find a sudden solution for a problem as tangled as Ireland's was. Yet another answered, saying that things would never change, for the Irish would never unite.

The crew that came in were wet and cold and they trudged off to their houses. There was as little warmth in the rest of us there either, for the cold of the evening was so severe.

'There is little use putting fishing gear together,' says a man, 'so long as the country is not at peace, nor anywhere near it.'

'There were five companies from England coming to this Island buying lobsters before the Great War in France broke out,' says Séamaisín, 'and I'm afraid not one of ye will live to see that again, however quickly or slowly peace may come to Ireland.'

However often before they had disagreed with what Séamaisín said, this time not a single man contradicted him.

January 1922

The House of Parliament

SEA and sky are in turmoil, slates fly off houses from time to time, sheds and the animals inside are being swept away together and there isn't a scrap of fodder to toss to any animal.

Diarmaid's house is the debating chamber they have now and, since they have no work of any kind to go on with, the whole company congregate there day and night. There is no question however hard, but someone would speedily solve it and, though they have neither scholarship nor great learning, no oversight in the law will escape their notice. And while Dáil Éireann is on the horns of a dilemma these days, it seems to me, trying to find a solution to many problems, the knottiest of them would soon be settled in Diarmaid's House of Parliament.

'. . . The labourers and workers, who are not gentlemen and have no means of becoming so, stand in need of the extra shilling to live. Why is it that the extra is not taken from those above them, who have money to spare and the King's roast thrown in, and from shopkeepers, who make a hundred pounds profit on every hundred pounds' worth of goods—instead, all the charges are levied on the country folk and on the land which supports the entire neighbourhood? The shopkeeper is a free agent but the countryman is forced to pay him any price he cares to ask for every item.'

If a man from Dáil Éireann were in this House of Parliament he would be greatly enlightened on matters about which he was ignorant before.

Spring 1922

Tadhg's rick

THERE is no rick of turf in this Island but the one belonging to Tadhg the Joker. It has been under a cover of scraws during the year and not a drop of rain touched it. He kept away from it himself as long as he could, because he knew that once he opened it, the whole village would be looking for a chance to help themselves to a bag or a bundle out of it.

Now, this morning he had hardly enough turf in the house to boil the kettle. As a result he had to fix panniers on two asses and set off towards the rick. He intended to take no rest day or night until he had the whole rick home, leaving no scrap of it for anyone else's benefit.

When he opened it he filled his two loads on his two asses, with a lad helping him, and they turned towards home. They meant to make three trips, that is six loads.

There was another man on the hill with his own ass and he was watching for his chance until Tadhg was out of sight of the rick. Then he went and filled a load on his own ass, at his ease. He headed for home after throwing his old coat on top of the load. Tadhg and the lad met him on the way back up, but thought nothing of it until they came to the rick.

That was when the fun started!

Spring 1922

'Strikes on Road and Track!'

TADHG was holding forth and declared:

'By Our Lady, this country will never come to rights. Currachs have come in from the mainland today and not a pennyworth of provisions in the bottom of any one of them. Strikes on road and track! And nothing travelling! The countryside is as badly off today as when the Great War was being waged in France. But I suppose there is nowhere else as bad as that cursed town of ours. There are poor fishermen hanging about Dingle Quay now. Normally they would have a shilling, a half crown and a crown, maybe, for their catch every day and they in sore need of it. But they have not stirred from the harbour for a fortnight over that rabble blocking the roads. Striking would be all right once or twice, but every hour and every week!'

'The country was never so upside down before,' said a man who was in the house.

'Oh, on my body and soul, the country will never come to rights. This is how it will be, themselves tearing it apart,' said Tadhg. 'Spiller's boat landed flour in Tralee a couple of weeks ago to be brought by train to Dingle, but no man could be found for gold or silver who would be willing to put a hand to it. Today a ship went north hoping to fetch the flour to Dingle again by sea, or else take it back home to Cardiff.'

'There is a prophecy, so I've often heard,' said an elderly woman in the house, 'that tears would be shed over the grave of the Englishman yet.'

'That day is not far off, unless they change their tune,' said Tadhg.

Spring 1922

Leather

FOR three days there was no sign of Séamaisín on the strand amongst the other pensioners. He was searching where the 'Quebra' went down, to see if he might come across any bits of salvage. There was an exceptionally low tide and this Séamaisín knew. It struck him that he could search places it had been impossible to search ever since the ship was wrecked.

The first day Séamaisín went looking he came across a great pile of leather with no more fault or flaw than on the very day the ship went down. According to a bootmaker, there would be no deterioration in leather left under water for twelve years. I believe that.

Séamaisín brought home nothing he found, only a small bundle of grass on his shoulder, and no one knew where he had been either. He would have been a great simpleton if he gave any hint of it, which would bring all in the village there before and after him next day.

That is what Séamaisín was up to for three days, until the tide was returning to normal and he had searched every nook twice and three times over. He found three pairs of ready-made boots, and no such thing had been found at any time. He spent the third day hauling leather home from morning till night. He has made more in those three days than the Islanders have in the past three months. He had seven whole perfect hides, not to mention pieces.

After bringing the leather home he made for the strand where the seaweed was, and he had it gathered and some of it spread on the potato field ahead of the other pensioners. He leaves them all standing!

Spring 1922

Hunters Missing

IT was a stormy day and Maitiú set off west to Inishvickillaun to go rabbiting. The crew took only one loaf of bread apiece with them. Three men were in the currach. They intended to stay back there three days until they each had a good haul, but instead of only spending three days they have spent five, and sea and sky are raging. Six or seven days may pass before they can budge—perhaps not even then.

One of Tadhg's sons is there and Tadhg says it is unlikely they are alive, for the day they set off west was foul and threatening. Next minute he is saying that even if they are alive, they will die of starvation.

'Haven't they rabbits?' someone suggests.

'Oh,' says he, 'they would hasten their deaths unless they had something else to eat along with them. A fresh rabbit is the sharpest purgative a person ever took.'

'But doesn't a man live for twelve days without eating a bite,' says someone.

'I wouldn't believe that from the Pope,' says Tadhg, 'and by Our Lady, I can only think that they are not alive there at all, for I go up the hill every day to gaze across at the house on the far island and I cannot see a puff of smoke at any hour of the day.'

'That is not a good sign,' says someone else.

Spring 1922

The Figure of St. Bridget

St. Bridget's Day. When I lifted the latch very early in the morning, there the pair of waifs were on the threshold, the figure of a baby cradled in the little girl's arms and the lad along with her as a companion. For all I knew they had been there half the night. I had little thought of St. Bridget's Day when I opened the door, but I knew as soon as I saw the image of St. Bridget.[1]

When they came in and I had pulled on my clothes I took a good look at them. They were sister and brother and close relations of myself.

Then I asked them what they wished to have—money, an egg, bread, or sugar, and if I had mentioned gold too they would still rather have had the sugar. Then I gave a handful of sugar to each of them and on their way out they left me their blessing. No other couple called in during the day, although these two told me that another was doing the rounds.

Many a year, when I was young, there used to be six or seven couples going from door to door on this Island at a time when there was no tea or sugar or flour. An egg and a penny was what they normally received in those days. It is a great thing that no old Irish custom has disappeared entirely. They will increase and multiply from now on since the people have won self-government—provided they can agree.

St. Bridget's Day, 1 February 1922

[1] The image was made from a sheaf of straw with a lath across it to serve as hands, and wrapped in clothing.

'Unless God's Help is at Hand'

PEOPLE from the Island have been out on the mainland for over a week. By the look and appearance of today they will be spending more than another week there.

'By my baptism,' said Lítheach, 'you can be sure the people on the mainland are not the ones who are worse off. They are free to roam, even if they are reduced to begging for charity. It is different here, where there isn't a stone of flour in this whole Island today, and where people will be growing weak before long unless God's help is at hand.'

He was holding a big spade at the time, his first day digging the ground.

'There's no fear of hunger on yourself, God bless you,' said a man going by while he was saying this.

'You won't see me here at all tomorrow unless the day is calm.'

'Why?' asked the other man.

'I have an empty belly, by my baptism, that's why!' said he, 'and I would have to have it full to work this big spade.'

'Perhaps tomorrow may be calm. The March storm is variable. It can be battering the houses down in the morning and be calm in the evening. See how the Dingle trawlers are suffering from the bad weather in the bay since morning.'

'They are, the poor men!' said Lítheach, 'and they in need of a shilling.'

'Even if they caught anything, either the railway workers would be on strike or the train would be out of order. There will always be something or other to thwart them. How well it is the poor man who suffers always, whatever reason there is for it,' said the other fellow.

'Yerra, man, you don't understand a thing!' said Lítheach. ''Tis a waste of my time talking to you! It is not the same case at all for the man whose pockets are bulging, when it comes to weathering the storm.'

March 1922

A Herb for every Disease

IT is a March day and it is living up to its name. Bad as it is, six vessels have gone through the Sound from the north, the sea washing in and out of them. Showers of hail and a gale of wind battering at them. People from this Island have been outside on the mainland for a fortnight and will be for another while longer if we are to believe what we hear. No potato or set has been planted here nor will be for some time to come, because no one can put his head outside the door.

Three days ago there was one man whose head had swollen for lack of tobacco; today there are four with the same disease, and their skulls the size of pots. If they had this herb, their heads would be cured in no time, according to Tadhg, for he had often suffered from the same disease himself. 'Their heads would be dried out before they had one pipeful of tobacco smoked,' said he.

'It seems there is a herb and cure for every disease, so, Tadhg,' said I.

'Is it how you imagine there is not?' said Tadhg. 'The devil take me, there is, wisha, if people could only find it. If you pricked every swollen head these have with the point of a knife, a full can of water would pour out, and that would not be there if they always had enough of what they need—plenty of tobacco.'

'Aren't there four old women in their beds for a week,' says Nell. 'How well no one has any pity for them.'

'Oh, wisha,' said Tadhg, 'may none of them live to see Sunday!'

'May God not heed you!' says she.

March 1922

Trawl-lines without Fish

THERE is a strong spring tide running. All the Islanders are out up to their necks gathering black seaweed. The days are fine for it too. The name we have for this spring tide is Ireland's Mouth on St. Patrick's Day. It seems as if it bears that name since the time of St. Patrick, for I heard it when I was a child.

Only about a hundredweight of potatoes have been planted here up to now and they were planted this very day. People have scattered east and west but the young men here would rather go onto their football field on the strand than into any potato field. That is natural to them, for as they grow up it is by the sea's edge that they are to be found.

Currachs were out fishing with nets last night. They had the bait for the trawl-line and they did bait it, but they have spent a long spring day in the middle of the bay and they haven't caught enough fish for one man.

'By Our Lady, my friend,' said Séamas, who watched them coming in empty-handed, 'the very fish in the sea have died off. Six hundred hooks, baited with mackerel, and they paid out there in the middle of the bay since day brightened, without catching so much as one fish to grill on the tongs!'

'You were used to the time of the Great War in France,' said Séamaisín, when there was twenty pounds worth of fish on every cast of the trawl-line.'

'Surely, 'tis the same sea still,' said another man.

'It is, but it is not obliged to make you a gift of twenty pounds every day,' said Séamaisín.

March 1922

Ill-equipped for Work

WHEN I think it is time for me to wander out I gaze all around the slopes of the Island. I lean back against a sheltering field wall and have my pipe going full blast. My God prosper the understanding man that made me the gift of what's in it.

It is many the day I have spent on this Island. Here I cut my teeth and here I lost them again except for the few of them I still possess. During all my time here, I thought that I had never seen the Islanders so feeble and so slovenly in making their living as I saw them now.

A man came along with an ass, harnessed with a packstraddle from which a sack was slung full of something. I had no notion what that was until he made straight for a handful of potatoes he had planted, and up-ended the sack. What was it but manure! That is the tinker's trick for spreading manure on potatoes. Many other asses were drawing manure but they were all equipped with a pair of panniers.

After making a great wonder of the man with the sack and his ass, the next thing I saw was a big, lanky, lean, bewhiskered fellow who had a coarse sheet slung on his back. He was toiling away drawing manure by this means. I don't know whether it was poverty of spirit or poverty of pocket that brought this about, but I had never seen anything like it before. The little ass would always be well harnessed for his task, however poor the master.

March 1922

Bringing home the furze. On the right is Maurice Kearney son of 'the Yank'. Taken from above 'the Yank's' house near the well at the top of the village

Ravages Wrought by the Storm

I Passed the three score years long ago and it is many the storm I rode out during that time on sea and on land, but the night that just passed made me think a hard day had never struck before. My son and myself were asleep when the gale woke us and we jumped out of bed, for stones and pieces of wood were hurtling about. But when we rose we were not able to open the door; all we could do was sit down and wait for day to brighten. At dawn the wind had slackened and veered westerly. It had been blowing from the south before.

When we went outside we found that the door fastened on the turf shed had been wrenched off and its roof had been swept clear away west onto the White Strand.

When I looked higher up the hill, the hen house belonging to the neighbour above had vanished. The cowshed and the cow herself were gone. The roofs had been blown all over the fields.

Off he went in search of the cow but he failed to find her, alive or dead. When he came back without her, his Sunday suit and every other stitch he possessed had been swept away! Off he rushed again looking for the cow and found her in the shelter of a gable end, barely able to stand.

As he was coming back with the cow, Seán Léan was calling to him to come to his aid, shouting with all his might while all the time the gale was blowing his house away. The other man could not go to his aid for the cow's legs had given way and he had to help her to get home. When he arrived back the chimney on his house had been blown down.

A big plank was missing from one of the other houses and the woman there was on her two knees beseeching God to calm the wind, at the same time shaking holy water in every direction. Every gust that struck the house swept another plank away.

This had been going on for some time but there was no sound

coming from her husband and she thought it odd. In the end she went up to the kitchen but there was no trace of him there. She thought he must have gone outside and that his days were ended. She moved to the window and called out. He made no answer. She called again and again. At last she thought she heard a feeble voice but she had no notion where the sound was coming from. She called louder.

'Where are you? Is it alive or dead you are? The sound is coming from somewhere inside. Surely if you were alive I would see you.'

'Yerra, woman, it isn't dead I am,' a rather faint voice said again, and by now she had searched every corner of the house so thoroughly that she couldn't have missed even a sod of turf, while from time to time another piece of the house flew away.

'Holy Mary, there is no slackening in it yet,' said the feeble voice again, and that was the moment when the man of the house put his head out of the cupboard.

He was no fool, but she was a featherbrain.

March 1922

Toil in Springtime

THIS is no day of idleness among the Islanders. The seven cares of the mountain are weighing on their shoulders. From All Hallowtide onwards they had tramped from one house to another, expounding points of law, mingling fact with fancy. Now, however, one of them would scarcely greet you on the road, they were so zealous for work. I saw a man on his own, digging with his spade in the early morning. Before long the strand was calling him. He hurried off and waded out up to his neck gathering seaweed with a sickle and rope, until the tide drove him back in. He carried the seaweed up the cliff to load on the ass. He came home, swallowed whatever was in front of him for dinner—and a hungry man who is working hard does not care whether the bite he eats is sweet or bitter. Then he headed out for the hill, gathered furze for kindling and drew a load of turf as well; he was no sooner home than he set off west to draw his seaweed; he spread it, covered it with earth and had the evening star for company on the way back. If he did not sleep that night it is a wonder.

The Great Blasket is a place of much hardship for a man on his own in a house, for during the winter there is nothing he can do that would be of help to him in the spring. Therefore he is faced with the need to do all the work at once. If he has lobster pots at sea he has to go out twice a day to attend to them. No sooner has he come in than he must start up the hill and put in a stint cutting turf. His bite of food is hard-earned.

March 1922

Tadhg's Opinions

Tadhg calls in looking to see if the *Misneach* journal contained any news of peace in Ireland, or was there any thought of giving relief to the poor of the country. According to Tadhg, there are no poor people in it except fishermen—'his own craft is the theme of every poet and prophet.'

'It isn't worth reading, Tadhg. Elections will be held again throughout Ireland. The two sides have split apart and they will have to come together.'

'By Our Lady, long ago someone said to me that if Ireland was completely free, the Irish would not keep control of her. O Mary Mother, all the poor people, carrying the begging-bag on their backs and all this while pinning their hopes on the politicians—what will they do now? The begging-bag is still there and, judging by all the signs, there it will always be,' says he.

'It is no use anyone passing judgment on them, Tadhg. Seeing that it has always been the way with the people of Ireland to split apart whenever anything favourable was within her grasp, what will happen now should cause no wonder either.'

'Yerra, and don't they say that the Treaty they brought back was wonderful, man, if we can believe what we hear; and, by the devil, if it was, what robbed them of their senses so that some would accept it and some would not?'

'If England spent seven years doing nothing but make a treaty for Ireland's benefit, there would be some of us who would not be satisfied.'

'Let them go to the devil, so, and to the west of Ireland!' says he.

April 1922

The Women Minding the Baby

THERE is a new baby in one of the village houses after the night. The midwife comes, stays until morning and takes herself off home to catch up on the sleep she has lost.

Now, whatever customs have died away, the customs following the Good People[1] have not, and so a couple of elderly women had to be found for the night, to make sure that the child would still be there in the morning. A roaring fire was blazing; food and drink were provided. The pair minding the baby were handed a pipe apiece and all the tobacco they could smoke. If I know them, more was spent on keeping the two pipes puffing than on the christening.

However dear the whiskey, there is no house like this without a drop, but these two women did not get a taste until day brightened, for fear the child might be stolen from them, if they were fuddled with drink at all. When the man of the house rose in the morning the baby had not been stolen away.

'Fetch that bottle there and give a drop of it to these women,' says his wife.

'They have earned it,' he said, 'they'll have the parting glass now.'

He fetched the bottle that was still unopened. He poured out a drop for them and a generous measure for himself.

April 1922

---

[1] The fairies.

Deaf and Dumb for Lack of Tobacco

I TAKE a stroll between two showers and a rare thing it is to find that respite at the present time. I cannot recall weather like this in the whole of my life, no more than the man born twenty years before me can recall it either. The Islanders have been on holiday for almost the entire year. They cannot go fishing. They have nothing to do on land. A man who had lost a leg from the hip down would have no trouble handling the amount of potatoes planted by the man who planted the most. I often saw twice the quantity of potatoes put in the ground on the mainland by a cripple leaning on a crutch!

Well, on my stroll round at this time who should come along but Dónall.

'God save you, Dónall.'

'God and Mary save you,' says he, 'isn't this the bad weather we're having?'

'There is not much to be said for it, surely,' says I to him. 'Have you managed to see to your few potatoes yet, Dónall?'

'Oh, I have given up trying, because the seed potatoes are rotting in the ground,' says he. 'Would you have any slice of tobacco in your pocket? Give me a taste of it if you have. I'm deaf and dumb for three days for want of a bit.'

I put my hand in my pocket and gave him some. I would make no boast of that, even if he was a man I had never laid eyes on before, leave aside the fact that he is my own uncle's son.

'You may as well head for the Poorhouse the day you run out of tobacco for yourself,' says I to him.

April 1922

Leaving for America

THE men of the village are on the strand today gathering loose seaweed—red seaweed it is called around May, for the creeks fill up with it at this time of the year. They are manuring turnips with it, for the handful of potatoes they have sown have been manured already. The hills are as white as milk still and there is thick driving hail today that would put out your eye. It is to be feared that an old woman from the village has lost the sight of one eye as a result of it too, after a hailstone struck her right in the eyes.

A young girl who is leaving for America was setting out. The usual custom is for all the people of the village to follow the emigrant down to the sea, and that's all that is left for them to do. It was while the old woman was accompanying her that the hailstone struck her in the eye.

It was at Ram's Cove that she had to be lifted into the currach. This was the spot where a lady visitor had to be lifted on board some years ago because the weather was so bad.

An enquiry has come to the Blasket from someone in County Clare for a girl who would improve his knowledge of Irish, write and read letters, speak it and teach it. That is not the case with Brian O'Kelly, of course. I don't know whether anyone else in the country has as much written Irish in front of him as he has to hand.

Wouldn't it delight my heart to be able to read a book of my own before I died.

April 1922

A Woman in Search of an Ass

THIS is a fine day. There will be a fair of some kind in Dingle tomorrow. It is a joyless day for me because many of the young people of this place have gone across, including my son, Séan, and he is all the company I have. That left me like an ill-sitting hen, up and down, myself and my work in disarray. Whatever task I set about was only half done and such work has to be started all over again—a rare case with me.

The crews of a couple of currachs have been out rabbiting on the small islands since day brightened. As fish is not to be had, there is little relish to go with the potatoes. Even rabbit is better than nothing. A currach with sheep from the Island has gone to the fair too. According to the butchers, there is no sweeter mutton to be found than a good sheep from the Blasket.

After eating half a dozen potatoes for the dinner, with a mackerel taken out of pickle—maybe if it was not a Friday I would have a pig's trotter or something—I went out for a little stroll. As I was on my way back a woman came towards me carrying a white bag to fetch some sand.

'You didn't see my ass at all in your travels?' says she.

'I did not.'

'I'll go home again so,' says she.

She turned back and found the ass braying with hunger in the little stable. He had been there since yesterday without being let out, because the man of the house was away on the mainland!

April 1922

A Man from the Island Selling a Cow

WE have news today from Dingle fair. A man from here had crossed over with a cow to sell, a poor-looking beast that even so looked better than she was, for she had not been able to chew for a couple of years on account of her toothless gums. He arrived in the market early because he had lodged in the town the night before. He had been standing in the fair-field for a while before anyone approached him. That was just as well, for when the jobbers came up they scattered what sense he had and it was little enough already. A strapping middle-aged man came up:

'What class of an article is that you have?' he asked.

The man with the cow stared at him and said:

'Isn't it all equal to you, the devil to it, what class she is, since you're so blind you can't tell whether she is a cow, a horse or a sow. You sound like an old ship's cook that never set foot on dry land until today!'

'You've been drinking a drop, man,' says the jobber, swishing his cane and leaving him there.

Another jobber was not far away and he came over.

'What are you asking for that rake?' he asked.

'She is a rake, surely,' says my man, 'and another rake has no need of her.'

'Faith, I'm no rake,' says the other fellow.

'That's the proper name for the likes of you, and not for a fat beast,' the man from the Island rejoined.

A Dingle man it was that bought the beast from him for two pounds.

April 1922

Seagulls' Eggs

Two currachs went out looking for seagulls' eggs, for their laying season is while the oats are being sown and just after. Any grain left on the surface they would gobble up. They usually lay three eggs—but two and four are often found in a nest.

The crews had baskets for bringing the eggs home and they were full when they returned in the evening.

One of Tadhg the Joker's sons had a full basket of them. When his father caught sight of all the eggs, here is what he said:

'I swear to the devil but they're the poultry that cost nothing to keep and it's little flour or meal they have swallowed for two years past, a far cry from the useless collection of hens in this house that gobble half a bag of meal every month.'

Tadhg put down a good turf fire. He took a large tin vessel with a loop-handle and filled it with eggs. When he judged that they were boiled he lifted them and put them in a basin in the centre of the table. Supper was going on at the same time.

'Well,' says he, 'if everyone does not have his fill of eggs tonight he never will. God's gifts are many.'

I happened to be in their house at the time—and the share of my life I spend there is not the most tedious part. Tadhg reached into the basin and took out an egg. It was not to his liking and he pitched it out of the door. Inside the next one there was a chick.

There was not a single new-laid egg in the basin.

'To the devil with my share of them!' says Tadhg.

May 1922

The Women and the Crows

I LEFT the house and when I reached the field where the ass was, I met Donncha there. We stretched out on the green herbs under the sunshine and we were discussing the letters that had come to all of us from visitors seeking a place to stay on the Great Blasket.

Suddenly two women screamed above our heads and we jumped up to see what the matter was. Donncha's own wife was there along with Diarmaid Bán's wife. They said that something had fallen down the cliff beneath us.

By the time we wound our way down, a throng of people had gathered and what was it but a stocky lad who had fallen down onto the White Strand. He had a couple of gashes. He had come through it harmlessly enough.

The lads had found a crow's nest in which she had two fledglings as big as herself. They had a rope to bring them away and a big long rod with a snare at the top to slip over the heads of the fledglings.

It was the women that had clubbed together to give a reward to whoever would remove the birds and their nest. They had their reasons for this, because by the end of a week the crows had left no hen, duck or any other domestic fowl around the houses. One woman lost her chicks; another had been robbed of her goslings.

'By my life,' says an old woman, 'didn't the old crow make to peck the eye out of my head!'

May 1922

Little Micilín's Conversation

I MET little Micilín out in the fields. Although Micilín is only a child he puts on airs to appear like a grown-up. I put a question to him. 'Did your brothers catch any fish the last night they went out?'

'They caught five hundred and stored them away to add to the next night's catch, always supposing there was any. They meant to take it to Dunquin then for carting to market in Dingle.'

'But did they catch anything the second night?'

'They went on the fishing bank all right but they were very thankful to God that they were able to make it home after all the wind and sea.'

'What did they do with the first catch then, Micilín?'

'When Éamonn rose in the morning he went down to the harbour where the fish were stored in bags. They had gone soft and the bellies were slimy. He untied the rope from each sack and threw every fish back into the sea where it came from.'

'Wasn't it a great shame to let it go with the sea when the neighbours have nothing for relish but salt.'

'We had no salt ourselves for preserving it, and the people who have would rather use that for relish than the fish,' says he. 'There are three fishermen in one house in the village who would not go out fishing at all, for they prefer to eat the salt.'

''Tis how God will put a stop to it altogether, Micilín.'

'He may as well,' says he.

May 1922

News from the Mainland

THE King crossed over to the mainland. Whenever he has an important task in hand he takes his time until he has it completed. Then he saunters down the main road in full view so that everyone can see him—everyone, that is, who might have business on the mainland himself. They cannot fail to see him and, since his currach is conveniently available, he is seldom without a crew for it, which is most convenient for him too. His pay is waiting for him on the table on the mainland and he does not look askance at it, although there is many a King all over the world who would have a nosebleed at the thought of earning a day's pay. But if they have no sense, our King here has no remedy for them.

On the mainland they heard that the farmers were driving each other off the land. One man had his horse harnessed ready for ploughing and they drove him out—the same is happening all over Ireland.

' 'Tis ever said that there will be tears shed over the grave of the Englishman yet,' says one man on the journey back to the Island.

'People have been crying for a long while after that rogue,' says another man in the currach.

'What these fellows are,' answers the King, 'are rogues like himself the Englishman had in this country, robbing poor honest people.'

'They're crying now because the old dancing-master has failed them,' says another man. 'The devil sweep them on all sides!'

'May you keep up the prayers and may God answer you!' says the third man.

June 1922

A Blasket Islander

Expectations are Often Disappointed

THERE are many fields in the land of Ireland but not one of them is like this one. This field can give a very good yield if it is put to work but that is not in the sinner's power.

In this field you have a view towards the four quarters and what the eye will not see the ear will hear, so that the man who comes working here is hindered from doing any work or task. Tomás O'Crohan is its owner. I am Tomás and it was the Congested Districts Board that gave it to me in the division of the land.

Well, I have been very much behindhand this year. A hundredweight of potatoes I have planted here have not been earthed up yet and I decided this day to limber up the old bones in order to do some work on the potatoes.

I prepared the morning meal for myself—a pint of good strong tea, a couple of large eggs, and butter too. I said to myself that it was a great help to the old bones to have proper food inside the body for tackling the great work I was about. I picked up a spade and shovel. I reddened my pipe and set off from the house.

Expectations are often disappointed. When I reached the field I stripped down to my shirt and set to work. It was not long before I heard a siren being sounded and I thought it must have been heard throughout the length and breadth of Ireland.

The ship was not visible yet but soon it came into view—a big American vessel. I did not take my eye off her until she passed out of sight rounding Cúl le Beann northwards and no king or knight ever had a ship more splendidly equipped.

I made another attempt to take up my implements again to catch up on the amount of the day I had lost—something I never had the opportunity of doing in this field, unlike every other field around.

It wasn't long—and now I was eager for work—before the voice sounded in my left ear, a voice that soon made me lay aside the shovel and brought my work to a stop:

> 'I'd grant her the palm of all beauty,
> But for Ireland I'd not tell her name.'

That was the song that was being sung and when I raised my head what did I see but four young women, ripe for marriage. You would think the singing came from one mouth and whatever the state of my old bones I would have been happy to follow them for three miles.

There were four more behind them and four others bringing up the rear. It was down towards the roadway of the White Strand they came. Each of the twelve had a white kerchief under her arm and the groups were about ten yards apart. No man alive could make any preference between them.

It was little work I managed to do that day!

June 1922

The Bull Seal

THERE were two men out in a currach and one of them dropped the other at a seal cave. He had a good stick and he moved in towards the end of the cave where he could see a great bull seal. The seal took no notice except to snarl at him. The man with the stick kept advancing towards him but he was making no move. At last, when the man judged he was close enough in to fetch him a blow with the stick, he struck him and the bull fell back belly uppermost.

He closed in on him then, to see if he would have any chance of dragging him towards the currach. He caught him by a flipper and was hauling him along until he came to a boulder blocking his way. He made an extra effort now, for once he had him on the other side of it the day was won.

When the seal saw that he was to be dragged over the boulder, he threw back his head, seized the great thick stick of red deal in his mouth and chewed up every bit of it as fine as snuff!

That filled the man with shivering black dread and he called to his companion in the currach to take him off. In the evening as they were turning for home they met another currach with five men aboard. The pair told them that a bull seal was laid out in the cave in there and with their help they might be able to carry it away. They hurried in at one another's heels, but the seal was as alive as he had ever been. They say he is a magic seal.

August 1922

Two Loads of Seals

WHEN I came home in the evening after the travels of the day, it reached my ears that there were two currachs in the harbour full of seals. I gave little credit to the first account, until the same story reached me again. Out I strode and headed straight for the cliff top.

The story was true. The two currachs lay as low in the water as they would be at manuring time in the spring when loaded with mussels. The whole village had gathered there. Old women, who for some time had not been able to move around, even in the house, without the aid of a stick, had arrived on the scene, and the young people were astonished to see them. The old women were eager to see again this sight that belonged to the old days.

There were seven full-grown seals and five young in one currach. In the other were five full-grown seals and three young. A bull seal in one currach was ten feet long and in the other were two bulls eight feet long. They would hardly have been lifted out of the currach yet but for all the willing hands that were gathered round.

September 1922

The Class of Vessel that Carried Máire to America

THERE is no spectacle more thrilling than to be watching ships ploughing the ocean through a storm. There were fifteen of them following in the wake of each other in the Blasket Sound today before dinner time, the smoke from every funnel rising to the clouds. A ship sinks down half her depth and then rises again, bringing a mountain of sea water on board. The water cannot drop back again for the gap is closed, so the ship flings the water cascading off on every side again. They sail slowly when the waves are high, for fear the ship might plunge too deep at full speed and not be able to steer herself up at will. One was so vast that you would think a mountain had collapsed into the sea every time she dipped her nose downwards.

'Holy Mary!' says a middle-aged woman, as she stood in the open doorway, with a child cradled in her arms, 'that's the class of vessel, I dare say, that carried Máire to America.'

'She is big,' says a strapping Yank, who had travelled over there and returned, 'but the ship that carried Máire could tow this one behind.'

The people of the village ate no dinner that day, they were so engrossed in gazing out at the vessels ploughing through the current of the Sound where sea and wind and spring tide were against them.

October 1922

Whatever happened to the Fish?

'DINGLE trawlers out fishing in the bay from morning to night and coming home without even a fish to grill on the tongs! King of the Saints! Whatever has happened to the fish of the sea?' says a woman on the Blasket, after the currachs had come in three nights in a row without herring or mackerel.

'I suppose, Mom,' says a lad she had by the hand, 'it is the big fishes that are eating the little ones.'

'My pet,' says the mother, 'even the big fish are no longer caught or seen. The trawl-line below at the bottom of the sea is without any fish, big or small.'

'There won't be any fishermen left in Ireland so,' says Siobhán, her daughter.

'There are precious few left already, and those won't stay. What is to keep them here?' says the mother.

'They will have to leave for America so,' says Siobhán.

'They do not find it easy to go there either. They need to have fifty pounds—a sum no fisherman has when he has spent the last three years without making a single pound.'

'Whatever are they to do so?' says Siobhán.

'I suppose they will have to become beggarmen,' says she, 'and there is every sign that more besides the fishermen will be in need of charity, Siobhán pet, as there's no peace in the country for any proper scheme to be set afoot that would keep Christians at home supporting their families.'

'Before long maybe life might improve, with God's help,' says the young woman.

October 1922

Two Days before Christmas

IT is wild and gusty today. People are gathering green branches to decorate the windows—ivy and other evergreens. The houses have been without a daub of paint or whitewash since last summer. There was not a crumb of lime to be had in Dingle since the train stopped running. Many another item is not to be found, and no means of procuring it. I am writing this on the Saturday before Christmas. Christmas Eve tomorrow. The people who have gone out to the mainland have not returned yet on account of the bad weather.

'Maybe,' the children say, 'the bad weather will ruin the Holy Night.'

The people of the village have made a trip to the hill and a sheep for well nigh every household has been slaughtered. I suppose those who have such delicacies will share them with the neighbours. The established custom is for them to share—except that we are seeing many changes in the world now, where there were none for a long time.

Women drove asses to the White Strand in the evening, carrying bags to fill with sand. You can take my word for it that they came very close to being cut off there till morning, sheltering under an over-hanging rock. There were women among them who had left young children behind at home. They were at their wits' end trying to get away, but it was beyond their powers. There was thunder and hail, and a gale was blowing. The old men had to go to their rescue and they had a struggle to make it back home, the weak and the strong together.

'They should not complain, seeing how the great sea did not pour in on them,' says Tadhg.

Before Christmas 1922

The Lone Woman's Talk

IT was the morning of Christmas Eve and I was going to the well to fetch a bucket of the invigorating water. I was delighted to have it there in plenty before me and every other poor sinner, whatever kind of beer the rest of the human race might have to drink.

I gave thanks to God too that I had my sight and that my limbs were working without the aid of a walking stick. I had no twinge of pain in my side and I was able to carry my bucket to the house, although this is my sixty-seventh Christmas tacking east and west.

When I came in sight of the well I turned and saw a middle-aged woman standing in a doorway, her two hands pressed against the jambs as she looked out over the sea. Says she:

'Great thanks to God that gave ye this day, in honour of the day the Son of God came on earth. Last night was battering down the houses and the hills . . . And,' says she again, 'look how He saw the unfortunate people of this Island caught in a trap, some of them forced to stay on the mainland for ten days, the rest on tenterhooks to go out and bring back some festive fare to mark the Holy Night.'

I stood still all the while this praiseworthy talk was going on, for I am no noisy loudmouth to interrupt the good woman, with her eyes on God, her children round her and their father across the Sound at this time, to bring some fare back to them in honour of Christmas Eve.

Now, when the good woman stopped speaking and had turned away from the sea to take another look up the hill she noticed me.

'Holy Mary!' she exclaimed, 'is it calm enough for the currachs to make it out to the mainland?'

'Where are they?'

'Oh! Look, six of them out there,' she said.

I was standing where I had no view of the sea until she spoke. Nor was I expecting any such thing so early in the morning. I took two quick paces forward until I had a clear view of the ocean. I saw the six under their six sails two-thirds of the way across the Sound and I did not take my eye off them until they all reached the landing place on the mainland safe and sound. All this while I could see no currachs, only their sails, for the sea was high.

'They're safe and sound on the mainland, my honest woman,' says I.

'Well, that is a good place for them to be, but I suppose they will be there still on New Year's Night.'

'Don't think that, my good woman. God didn't give them the start of the day to make prisoners of them at the end of it. 'Tis better the day will be getting, you'll see.'

'May God speak through your mouth!' she said. 'Now go and fetch your water for the day,' which I did.

Before Christmas 1922

New Year's Day 1923

BAD weather. At this time an old age pensioner was in need of the priest. A currach made a run out to the mainland to fetch him. The priest arrived at the harbour but a gale blew up, forcing him to go back home and the currach to stay outside until the following day. The priest was there again but he had to return home once more, although the currach reached the Island very late in the day with the sea sweeping over it.

The sick man was getting no better while, meantime, the crew were waiting for their chance to make another dash out; when it came, they seized it. The priest was in Dunquin before them, saying Mass on the first day of the New Year. He came along, although the day was not to be praised. The weather held up until he had been taken back out, but the crew paid for it on the return journey.

The old man is alive still. Now they are talking about the coffin for him, saying it cannot be brought in because they are so doubtful about the unsettled weather. Each day the great sea rises to the level of the fields. The sky is threatening.

'We're paying for the fine weather, boys,' says Séamaisín.

I am writing this at the start of the New Year in God's name, and if we spent the Old Year well, may we spend the New Year seven times better, with the support and help and love of God and of mankind. And, since our people throughout Ireland cannot understand each other, may God grant the grace of understanding to them before the year is long gone.